how to start a home-based

Dog Training Business

Peggy O. Swager

gpp®

Guilford, Connecticut

Spot art licensed by Dreamstime.com

Editorial Director: Cynthia Hughes Cullen
Editor: Tracee Williams
Project Editor: Lauren Brancato
Text Design: Sheryl P. Kober
Layout: Sue Murray

636.
7

Library of Congress Cataloging-in-Publication Data is available on file.

ISBN 978-0-7627-8004-4

Printed in the United States of America

10 9 8 7 6 5 4 3 2 1

With any small business, family support is always critical. My husband, Ken, has dealt with a lot of dog training, hauling dog equipment, and the occasional dog bite without complaint. We so often talk about giving dogs a forever home; I think Ken has earned his. My children, Scott and Tia, have also aided with my dog training endeavors, and still do as adults. And as always, I need to thank my mother for allowing me, as a youth, to work with all kinds of animals, which began the process of honing my skills in animal behaviors. To my totally supportive family, I dedicate this book.

Contents

Acknowledgments | xi

Introduction | xiii

01 The Diverse World of Dog Training | 1

Why Become a Dog Trainer? | 1

Is This Job for You? | 2

The Need for Dog Training | 3

Finding Your Niche in a Diverse Dog Training World | 4

Personal Journeys of Dog Training Success | 5

02 Before You Begin | 12

Training, Skills, and Knowledge Needed | 12

Your Support System—Everyone in the Family Ends Up Involved | 16

Friends Can Be Valuable Assistants | 17

Reaching Out to Others in the Dog Community | 18

Building Your Name in the Dog Community | 21

Avoiding Negative Dog Politics | 22

Mining Future Business—Treating All Dog Contacts as
   Potential Customers | 23

03 Create Your Home Office and Work Space | 24

Setting Up Your Home Office Area | 24

Do You Really Need a Home Office? | 25

Things You'll Need in Your Home Office | 25

Dog Area That Is Specific and Separate | 29

Convenances and Zoning | 30

Licensing and Permits | 31

Health Department and State Regulations | 31

Being a Good Neighbor | 31

04 Getting Down to Business | 33

Your Business Plan | 33

The Right Balance for Success | 38

What's in a Name? | 39

Your Logo and Business Image | 40

Obtaining a Website Address | 41

Business Structure Options | 44

Why You Need an Attorney | 47

05 Taxes and Record Keeping | 49

The Difference between Bookkeeping and Accounting | 49

What Is Cash Flow and What Is Accrual? | 54

Record Keeping | 55

Understanding Balance Sheets, Income Statements, and
    Cash Flow Reports | 60

A Healthy Perspective | 69

Expense Analysis | 69

Educational Help Outside of College Courses | 72

06 Insuring Your Success | 73

Homeowner Insurance Extensions or Independent Policies | 73

Automobile Insurance | 75

Liability Insurance | 75

Business Interruption Insurance | 77

Workman's Compensation | 78

Do You Need an Independent Insurance Agent? | 79

07 Banking on Your Future | 80

Checking and Savings Accounts | 80

Checks as Receipts | 81

Charge Cards and Credit Cards | 82

08 Financing Your Training Business | 86

What It Will Cost | 86

Small Business Loans | 89

Is Credit Card Financing Practical? | 92

Are Investors a Solution? | 92

Where to Buy Supplies | 93

Guidelines about Selling Merchandise | 94

Setting Your Prices | 94

09 The Basics of Working at Home | 96

Keeping Track of Paperwork for Your Clients' Dogs | 96

Notes When Doing Private Consultations | 96

Class Syllabus and a Contract for Training Classes | 100

Using the Computer—and More—to Your Advantage | 103

The Telephone—Fielding Potential Client Questions | 106

The Great Information Exchange | 108

Office Hours—Setting Parameters with Clients and Family | 109

10 Constructing Your Training Business | 111

Creating Training Areas at Your Residence | 111

Getting an Idea of the Size You Need for a Class | 113

Renting Facilities for Dog Training | 114

Facility Considerations | 115

Acquiring Needed Equipment | 115

Dealing with the Doo-Doo | 116

Building Your Reference Library | 116

Dressing the Part When Meeting the Public | 121

Dog Consultations | 122

Creating a Training Contract | 123

11 Marketing and Public Relations | 125

Building Word of Mouth | 125

Websites That Sell Your Business | 126

Using Social Media | 126

Business Cards and Brochures | 132

Advertising through Veterinarians, Groomers, and
    Doggy Day Care Centers | 134

Advertising through Print | 135

Dog Booths at Shows or Events | 136

Mailing Out Advertisements | 136

Mining Future Customers from Current Customers | 137

Gift Certificates | 138

A Few Last Tips | 139

12 Behind the Scenes | 142

Qualifications for Teaching Classes | 142

Other Education Needed in Trainers | 147

Places to Learn Your Skills | 147

What Is a Behaviorist? | 148

Certifications for Dog Trainers | 149

Organizations That Promote Specific Disciplines | 150

Rally and Agility Organizations | 151

Dog Training Schools | 151

A Petsmart or Petco Education | 152

E-Training | 153

13 Growing Your Business | 158

The Advantage of Starting Small | 158

Selling Equipment | 159

Offering Other Dog Services | 160

Adding Staff | 160

Hiring Employees Means Paperwork | 164

Paying Employees | 164

Hiring a Subcontractor or Independent Contractor | 166

An Important Note about Insurance | 167

The Family Factor with Small Business Employees | 167

Motivating Your Employees to Do Their Best | 168

Concluding Thoughts | 170

Appendix A: Roundtable Questions | 171

Appendix B: Dog Training Associations and Certifications | 183

Appendix C: Resources | 185

Appendix D: Sample Brochure | 187

Index | 188

About the Author | 192

Acknowledgments

Thanks to my agent, Rita Rosenkranz, for facilitating the opportunity to do this book.

To Linda Bollinger for sharing her in-depth knowledge of dog training and dog behaviors, and for being so willing to discuss some of my more difficult cases.

To Tia Reinschmidt for changing the course of my training from horses to dogs.

To Janice Dearth and Nannette Nordenholt who always have a wealth of information.

Introduction

Hardly a day goes by that we don't see something on television about dogs. On *Good Morning America,* you quickly find out that Robin Roberts has a Jack Russell. As well, George Stephanopoulos has mentioned his dachshund and his terrier mix. Did you know that Dr. Andrew Ordon on *The Doctors* has a bulldog? He talks about his dog every chance he gets. People we watch on the television are only reflecting our growing interest in canines. Dogs have, more than any time in our history, become an important part of our society. And you don't need to be a television personality to have caught the desire to show off and talk about your dog. While doing a book signing for my dog training book, *Training the Hard to Train Dog,* several people who stopped to chat were quick to show me photos they carry around, not of their children, but of their dogs. The role of the dog in the family structure has changed, and more and more people acquire one, two, or a pack of dogs, driving more of a need for dog training. In recent years, the push to adopt a dog from a rescue has also unleashed a surge for instructions to help when reforming canine behavioral problems. And don't forget that people are using dogs for activities such as agility or as a certified therapy dog used to visit a nursing home. All of this creates, more than ever before, a demand for dog trainers.

Being a dog trainer requires a diversity of skills. First off, you must have a desire to do this job, a bit of what one might call dog sense, and a knack for training. Those who pursue dog training as a career find that the ability to turn something you enjoy into a profession can have great rewards. For people who want to become a dog trainer, the first step is commitment. For people who want to begin a dog training business, they need to expand their education to include the details of running a small business.

I had two goals in writing this book: One goal was to empower people looking to start a dog training business with the information they need to plot a path for success; the other was to help people who have already started their dog training business, but found their journey not progressing as they expected, to discover the information they need to get back on the path to success.

Since some people may not yet know where they fit in when it comes to the dog training business, chapter 1 addresses finding one's niche in the diverse dog training world. Although every aspect and opportunity for dog training can't be covered, you will find I've covered in more detail the opportunities where people are more likely to earn a living. I did not limit the book to my experiences in dog training alone. You will find interviews from a variety of dog trainers who talk about their personal journey to dog training success.

Even before you begin your business, you will have a lot of decisions to make. The content of this book facilitates those decisions by letting you take a look at the pros and cons of different options. For example, you will learn information to help you decide if you should sell equipment. If you do decide to sell equipment to supplement your income, you will find out how to do so with a minimum investment, helping to keep your profits at a maximum.

Your dog training business will require different kind of permits as well as zoning considerations. If you want to hold classes away from your home, you learn what to look for in a rental facility as well as get an idea of how much space you will need. Included is information about insurance you need to secure for your business.

When looking to get your business off and running, you may find yourself halting at the business part of the business. Suddenly people are demanding a business plan. You find you have bookkeeping obligations and wonder about working with an accountant or a bookkeeper. To keep you from stopping your forward progress, the book takes you by the hand and walks you through the business end of dog training. You will not only find help in constructing your business plan, you will also find information to help you understand some of the financial sheets generated by a business, including profit-and-loss statements and balance sheets. You will even learn about cash flow projections and why they are valuable to you as you begin your business. Perhaps one of the greatest dangers in starting up a business is not starting at the right pace for success. An interview with an MBA helps you understand how to avoid this pitfall.

Small business success is more dependent on a good support group than a larger business. For many who are beginning a home-based business, that support group will be your family. I know my family was very important to my success and I readily share how to gather and work amiably with your home forces. I also help you learn how to draw on help from the community around you.

No matter how much desire or natural skills you have, you will find that being a dog trainer means you will embark on an endless educational journey on how to better train a dog. Even behaviorists find they need to specialize their studies when working to help resolve canine behavior issues. These days there are a lot of learning opportunities out there for dog trainers, but not all of those will be worth your financial investment or your time investment. This book gives you a lot of information to help you sort through educational opportunities and determine how to best guide your career. Included are certifications for different kinds of training.

Have you decided if you are going to be a sole proprietorship, an LLC, or do you need to consider becoming a corporation? The information provided will help you understand the different business structures, from sole proprietorships to corporations, as well as their advantages and disadvantages. You will also learn about times that you may need to consult an attorney.

What all do you need for a web page? Should you have a logo? What are the do's and don'ts when choosing a business name? These all need to be addressed early in your business endeavors. Those are part of your first steps toward marketing your business. More decisions will follow as you ask yourself questions like: Should you be on Facebook? Have a booth at the local dog event in your area? Mail out advertisements? Or is there a way to get a lot of customers without spending a lot of money? Since marketing is key to the success for any business, a lot of information is provided on what works when marketing a dog training business and what doesn't pay to invest in, from creating business flyers to engaging in different kinds of Internet marketing.

I worked hard to integrate both my dog training and my business experience. But I wanted you, the reader, to benefit from more than my personal experiences. So I took steps to bring you more information. You will find scattered throughout the book first-hand interviews from business experts and other experienced dog trainers. The goal of this book is to empower you with the info you need to succeed. If you know you want to make your living working with dogs, but are uncertain just where to begin, what area of dog training to pursue, and how to succeed, this book is designed to give you those answers.

I enjoyed the opportunity this book allowed to share my experiences, both good and bad, with the business of dog training. But I also wanted to take the opportunity to share others' experiences. My final unique contribution to this book was to interview three different successful dog trainers who are well along in their businesses' journey: one who had learned how to balance her job as a mother with her business; another who transitioned from a full-time job to owner of a dog training business that now supports her family; and the last who is now living a dream far beyond what she envisioned when she began her journey.

The Diverse World of Dog Training

The term "dog training" brings different pictures to people's minds. Some people see themselves in a role similar to television personalities such as Cesar Millan or Victoria Stilwell. But the world of dog training has a much greater diversity than one-on-one sessions with problematic dogs. Dog trainers are found in classes from puppy and agility, to Canine Good Citizen and therapy dogs. Some trainers specialize in training dogs for search and rescue or as aids for the blind or the deaf. There is truly a diverse calling for dog trainers. Since any dog training discipline takes education and experience, this book will not venture into more specialized areas such as how to train dogs to appear in movies, or even how to train a Seeing Eye dog. Instead, this book talks about how to begin your dog training career and how to make money in some of the more popular areas such as teaching basic classes and/or doing one-on-one consultations. So if you want to start a dog training business, or are looking to improve your current dog training business, you will find this book holds many valuable answers.

Why Become a Dog Trainer?

There are perhaps as many reasons to become a dog trainer as there are breeds of dogs. Although every dog trainer has his or her own personalized story, there are a lot of common threads as to why people choose to become dog trainers. A lot of people want to work with animals, oftentimes dogs in particular. So why not make a living at it? One of the advantages of becoming a dog trainer is that there are several areas you can specialize in, as well as the ability to move from one training discipline to another. You can even do several areas of dog training at once. For example, you may begin with obedience training because you like the discipline or may even like showing at obedience. Once you establish yourself as a trainer, you may decide to begin the journey to becoming a judge. Judging obedience doesn't exclude you from being an instructor, but it may help fill your classes. Some people who start out in obedience, may discover agility is more their passion. That may result in them teaching agility classes. Others may take a liking to Rally.

Perhaps you are interested in educating people on how to train their pets to become more manageable and mannerly. These classes start at the puppy class level and often follow the dog's development through the first year. By helping people train their everyday pets, you keep those same dogs from filling animal shelters where many animals are destined to be euthanized. Becoming a dog trainer can fill a need for the dog-owning public. At the same time, you can enjoy earning a living while working with dogs and their owners.

Is This Job for You?

Most people who succeed at this job have a passion for working with dogs. But to really succeed, you will need a bit more than that. With few exceptions, when you work with dogs you also need to work with people. If you absolutely hate dealing with people, you'll need to learn some techniques to make dealing with people easier. But take heart, you can learn these skills just as certainly as you can learn dog training techniques. In fact you may find that dealing with poorly behaved dogs has some parallels to dealing with difficult people.

With any business, there are certain keys to success. Typically in a smaller start-up business like dog training, you will need to wear many hats. You will probably be your primary marketing team and may also be your bookkeeper. Although this diversity of talents may make some people take a step backward, take heart. Inside this book, you'll find information and ideas to help you in all areas of starting up and succeeding in your business.

Most successful dog trainers have an aptitude for working with dogs. To help determine if you have that knack, ask yourself a few questions: Do I have patience with animals? Am I willing to dedicate myself to learning? Do I have an animal sensitivity?

So what is animal sensitivity? Animal sensitivity deals with an ability to understand an animal and what that animal is feeling. This can be helpful when working to reform canine behavior issues. Fortunately, you can learn how to be more sensitive to a dog. There are books and clinics on how to read a dog's body language. You can learn from others who have undertaken extensive studies to figure out what is going on inside the dog's head and what is driving a particular behavior. This kind of training was not always available. Little was documented about dog training before World War II and it wasn't until the 1990s that our dog training methods changed from jerking on choke collars to using operant conditioning. Now, there is a wealth of information that wasn't available even ten years ago.

Learning to be a successful dog trainer means learning about a diversity of dogs. Although a specific breed of dog is often characterized by a collection of behaviors, you will find that within a breed you can have differences in individual dogs. If those differences are driving unwanted behaviors in the dog, you'll find people turning to you as a dog trainer to help solve the issue. Likewise, you'll find that different breeds of dogs can have different learning styles. By learning several techniques and knowing the differences in breeds, you'll find yourself succeeding where others have failed. Although this obviously entails a lot of work, if this job is for you, you'll find yourself enjoying the life-long learning process.

A good question to ask yourself is: "Can I take on the right attitude for successful dog training?" That attitude is one that portrays self-confidence to the dog and to the dog owner. You must appear to a dog as a solid leader. Some people make the mistake of thinking that to help a dog, especially one that has suffered at the hands of misguided humans, we need to make up for any injustices done to the dog. That is not true. Although it is fine to have empathy for a dog, a good trainer learns how to use this constructively. To do good by an animal, you need to reach beyond your empathy and sympathy and find a way to help the animal. Sympathy doesn't change unwanted behaviors, even with a dog that has been abused. Dogs need guidance not coddling. But don't think for a second that doesn't mean you can't be a compassionate trainer. Harsh techniques are not necessary for changing unwanted behaviors.

The Need for Dog Training

Look around and you'll see that dogs have become an important part of our lives. We take them in our cars when we drive. We take them on our vacations or to special events. We've even designed dog parks for them. A lot of people consider their dog part of their family. Not only has the abundance of dogs in our society driven more need for dog training, the diversity of dogs has created needs. Dogs kept for pets come from a diversity of breeds, some of which were bred to do specific jobs such as herding or guarding. Unfortunately, dog owners don't always consider the needs or specialized training and exercise required for different breeds of dogs. After seeing a breed of dog on television or at the movies people decide to get one as a pet. The hit *101 Dalmatians* led to a surge in Dalmatian owners. The 1986 movie *Down and Out in Beverly Hills* did a lot to launch the popularity of Border Collies. More recently Chihuahua movies have created a surge in people acquiring this type of dog. Some of these suddenly popular breeds didn't work out for many dog owners. People didn't do the training or provide the exercise the dog needed. Finding their dog was out of control or destructive, the dog was turned over to a dog rescue or a dog shelter. This resulted in animal shelters and dog rescues quickly filling with unwanted pets. At one time this animal disposal technique meant a large number of dogs were euthanized on a regular basis. These days, both animal shelters and rescues often take an active role in trying to find unwanted dogs new and permanent homes. Many of these dogs will need a trainer to help straighten out some of their behavior issues so the dog can fit into a new home. With the popularity of adopting pets from shelters these days, there is more need than ever before for dog trainers.

Problem dogs or dogs lacking in adequate training are not the only places where you are likely to find the need for dog training. More than ever, people are enjoying doing things with their dogs. Dog shows are more abundant than ever before. More people are showing at obedience and Rally. Events like agility have become so popular they have their own shows through organizations such as North American Dog Agility Council (NADAC) and United States Dog Agility Association (USDAA). What all this means is that now, more than ever before, there is a higher demand for dog trainers to teach everything from more formal classes to events that are just plain fun.

Let's not forget that some dogs are still trained for specific jobs. Dogs are used in the field for hunting. They are also shown in trials to claim awards for their skills. Herding dogs can be found moving stock at a ranch or at a herding trial. While out hiking one day, I saw someone sitting at the base of a tree. Since this wasn't a usual place for someone to sit to pass time, I paid him a bit more attention than I normally would. He seemed, as best I could figure, a little bored. So I asked him if he was alright. He replied, "I'm waiting to be found." Then he explained he was helping in the training of a dog for search and rescue.

Finding Your Niche in a Diverse Dog Training World

Perhaps when you first toyed with the idea of becoming a dog trainer, you had a specific idea as to what kind of training you wanted to do, or perhaps you are less sure of exactly what area is your best fit. There are a lot of ways to find your place in the dog training world, and for some, their original idea may lead them in a direction they never imagined. One person started her dog training career teaching obedience. Then she began to teach canine good citizen classes. But she found her real calling in a therapy dog program where people and dogs became certified to go on nursing home visits. So no matter where you decide to begin your journey, keep in mind your first step on your dog training career may only be the beginning of a longer journey.

Personal Journeys of Dog Training Success

For some people the most challenging part of their journey will be figuring out where they want to go and how to get there. After all, this is a path you have never traveled. Yet to be successful you will need to envision parts of the journey. Below are a collection of dog trainer's personal stories to help you shape and reach your personal goals.

Janice Dearth, a Dog Trainer and More

Janice began her dog training experience at an early age. She began dog shows at the age of twelve and by sixteen, she began an apprenticeship at a dog training class in Ohio. By eighteen, she was teaching classes on her own. Back then, obedience classes were for showing in classes. Not until about ten years ago did the concept of pet training classes, often called obedience, really come into its own.

Janice felt she always had a knack for teaching and that it was something she really liked doing. She continued learning, apprenticing, and teaching which helped her in her own competition classes. Both the apprenticing and the teaching allowed her to experience different breeds and their variety of temperaments, as well as the different personalities in their owners.

In the mid-1990s she decided to diversify and became an obedience judge. She kept up with training classes while adding obedience judging to her resume. She got into Rally on the ground floor in 2000. This began a new passion and she has not only taught Rally, she is also a judge and has written a book on Rally. She is now trying a new direction, taking her training classes online by teaming with e-trainingfordogs.com.

Janice was recently approached by a woman who announced she was retiring from teaching and now wanted to become a dog trainer. Janice's first question was had the woman trained any dogs? To which the woman answered, only her own. Janice will tell you, as she did this woman, that hands-on experience is necessary to become a dog trainer/instructor. Although school teachers gain some of the necessary people handling skills, they need to gain experience with multiple breeds of dogs. Janice also emphasized that trainers need to make a name for themselves. Ironically, several years ago she ran into someone she'd taught in Ohio back at the very beginning. The woman had gone on to compete at the utility level. She said, "You were my first obedience instructor." Janice, now living in Colorado, found this to be an exceptional meeting.

Sue Brown, owner of Love My Dog Training

From an early age Sue Brown wanted to work with animals. However, when she went to college, she took accounting because she needed a job that could comfortably support her. After working a few years in accounting, she began volunteering for a humane society. Later she volunteered for the Dumb Friends League in their humane education and behavior departments. At first she used volunteer work as an outlet, a way to revisit her passion for animals, but later she decided this was what she wanted as a career.

Once Sue decided to go into dog training as a business, it took about three years for her to support herself. In the time between, Sue worked her regular job and did her dog training in the evenings and on weekends. By the time she was able to quit her day job, Sue's business, Love My Dog Training, was not only thriving, but due to economic issues, she became the only support for the family.

Sue doesn't rent a facility, but pays a percentage to vets' offices and other similar facilities. She also conducts in-home consultations. To facilitate her training education, she'll tell you she is fairly self-taught. Some of her knowledge comes from the vast resources of dog training and behavior literature and DVDs. Sue expanded her education by attending conferences and seminars as well as learning from and networking with other trainers. She became a Certified Dog Behavior Consultant (CDBC) through the International Association of Animal Behavior Consultants and a Certified Professional Dog Trainer through the Certification Council for Professional Dog Trainers. Sue feels she had a leg up on the business side of things having worked in a business-related field.

Steve Brooks, CPDT/KA, owner of Steve Brooks K9U

Steve Brooks didn't actively pursue dog training, instead dog training pursued him. Now, after twenty years, he finds this was the right job for him all along. A dog named Sven was responsible for his initial change in profession.

Steve was actively pursuing his music career as a drummer. The day he got to Nashville, he saw a dog thrown out of a moving car window. Steve didn't know anyone in the town, or any dog rescues, so he took the dog to the vet. At the vet's office, Steve found more than some help for Sven, Steve found a day job to help make ends meet while he pursued his music. But things didn't go as well for Sven at the vet's. Sven had aggression issues and lacked trust in humans. Due to his unpredictable temperament, many veterinarians recommended the dog be "put down."

Steve saw the good in Sven and he was determined to bring it out. Steve's dedication to training Sven led to the dog's reform. After a few years where he worked as a vet tech by day and a musician by night, Steve left his music pursuits and became a dog trainer at an established facility. The harsh techniques used by the facility didn't set well with Steve, so he began to go to conferences, seminars, and workshops where he learned and adopted positive training techniques. He became a Certified Professional Dog Trainer (CPDT-KA).

Steve relocated to California and has refined his skills and grown his business to include several aspects of dog training as well as classes. He started his dog training business and called it Steve Brooks K9U (aka K9U Dog Training). He likes to customize his dog training, claiming, "Like people, all dogs are different with different histories that influenced their behavior." Being near Hollywood, Steve enjoys working with stars with pet problems as well as an occasional opportunity to train a dog for media performances. His focus with his dog training is real-life manners, behavior problems, and teaching dogs tricks. He has expanded his business to include boarding, and also sells supplies, including holistic dog foods and practical training equipment clients may need. He has also taken on a couple of employees.

In 2005, Steve lost his beloved Sven. What Steve will never forget is how this dog, that so many people advised Steve to euthanize, had such a profound influence on his life. Steve has more information about Sven at his website, www .stevebrooksk9u.com.

Michelle Douglas, owner of Refined Canine

To say that Michelle's first dog came into her life when she was a very small child would be a bit misleading. That first dog arrived and was gone within weeks and her parents never had another dog. Dog ownership just wasn't their thing. Michelle didn't realize dogs were her thing until college when her boyfriend, now husband, gave her a Shar-Pei. Ever since, Michelle's life hasn't been the same.

The arrival of her first dog was responsible for Michelle changing her career from music to a field that involved animals. Her first thought was to be a veterinarian; unfortunately she hadn't taken biology or chemistry classes in high school, making the science classes required overwhelming. In college she took a behavior course and found her calling.

Shortly after college, she found out about the Association of Pet Dog Trainers (APDT) and it offered her a vast amount of information, from their magazine to their conferences. When she began her dog training business, Refined Canine, she maintained a day job. She taught classes out of a rented place, but that didn't work out well because of litter left by other renters. She changed to teaching through a recreation center, which worked out better because she could focus more on dog training rather than logistics. Soon, she began to consult on behavior issues. After she became pregnant with her first child, she found the day job had been replaced by the Mom job. Since she couldn't quit her Mom job to take on the business full time, she then began to supplement her income by becoming a subcontractor for another local training facility, while maintaining her own business teaching classes, offering private training lessons, and consulting for behavior issues. Michelle is always continuing her own education in behavior and training, teaching classes, doing behavioral consultations, and mentoring new trainers.

In 2010 Michelle was president of APDT. She felt this was a way to give back to the organization that shaped her as a professional. She feels this is a great group to network with, and although she did a lot of that before becoming president, she now realizes when she contacts people they now have a face to place with the name. She now offers an apprentice program to others for dog training.

Gail Fisher, owner of All Dogs Gym

Gail's dog training career has spanned forty years and she quickly describes her life as filled with serendipity. Gail's journey began with a vizsla she owned while working on Wall Street as an administrative assistant in the 1970s. Because Tisza barked when Gail went out at night, she received an eviction notice from her apartment landlord. To resolve the issue Gail hired a dog trainer. Through that experience, Gail discovered her calling. She moved to California where she apprenticed with a dog trainer and worked in a boarding kennel and grooming shop. In the 1970s, there were no formal training classes for dog trainers, leaving dog trainers to their own means of education. Gail's mentor was a wonderful dog trainer who, after a year, moved out of the area and bequeathed the training classes to Gail. Gail expressed her worry about being prepared for this level of responsibility, but with encouragement from her departing mentor, Gail found out she was ready and able to succeed.

When Gail and her husband moved to New Hampshire, they bought a small boarding kennel where she did training, boarding, and grooming. Like many groomers, Gail learned a lot about subtle canine body language, facial expression, pupil dilation, and slight changes in body tension.

Because there were no classes in dog training and behavior being taught anywhere at the time, to attempt to fill the void, and as part of her own educational journey, Gail developed and taught a two-year certificate program for dog trainers at the University of New Hampshire. Needing to study primary sources to stay one step ahead of her students, Gail looks back on this time as the most important educational experience of her life.

Throughout the 1980s, Gail grew her business to where she had classes in seven different locations in New England, and had several dog trainers who worked for her. At the time, a stand-alone facility for dog training was extremely rare. Trainers instead ran classes in such places as recreation buildings or church basements once a week. Frustrated with losing places for different reasons, and having to look for a different facility, Gail decided to rent a building that was exclusively for her dog business and found that endeavor very successful.

Over the years, Gail has done breeding, showing, competitive obedience and agility, and training dogs, from household pets to specialties such as dogs for the hearing impaired and service dogs, through a Prison Dog program. She is now in a permanent facility called All Dogs Gym and Inn (www.alldogsgym.com). She employs fifty-five people either part or full time. They do training, boarding, dog and puppy day care, as well as behavior modification.

My Story

Back in the early 1970s when I first went to college, my first goal was not animal behavioral studies, but to become a veterinarian. The world was a much different place back then. There were almost no female veterinarians to be found, and for every applicant to vet school, only one in seven was accepted. For women working to enter the field of veterinarian medicine, they found bias against them. The doors were not open like they are today. One of the requirements for applying to vet school was that you had some animal experience, so to expand my experience, I worked for free as a vet assistant. In those days there were no vet techs. The first program for vet techs was just opening up in Michigan State in 1973.

After applying for two years to veterinarian school without success, I began to look into other possibilities for my future. I was fascinated by animal behavior; unfortunately, there were almost no classes offered on the subject. After taking some time off, I transferred to a different college and took up biology as my major, hoping to find a way to work with animals. The only class even close to offering insight into animal behavior that was offered was called animal ecology, which only touched on animal behavior. So I took psychology classes and teaching classes to expand my education. I graduated in 1978 with a BS in biology and a minor in education.

To hone my skills with animals, I trained horses. In no time at all, I found myself working to resolve horse behavior issues. I wrote about a few of my experiences and got two articles published in a popular horse magazine. The first article talked about how training neurosis was created in a horse by using cues that were too similar for the horse to distinguish. The second article told how to use verbal cues to "hype" a horse for a speed event rather than the common technique of smacking the horse with a whip to get the horse revved up. My early education in horse training was littered with harsh training techniques, as was a lot of my dog training.

Making a living working with horses wasn't an easy task in those days, especially for a woman. After all, there were still rules against letting women show stallions in a show ring and the attitudes were slow to change. After I got married, I worked in research chemistry until the demands of a family meant I had to quit any full-time work. Over the years, I spent what time I could working problem horses. Although I'd had dogs since I was a kid, and did training of any dog, my techniques were old school and at times more harsh than they needed to be.

About twenty years ago, when my daughter was a teenager, she wanted a dog all her own, specifically a Jack Russell Terrier. We both ended up with a puppy from the same litter and I accompanied my daughter to many shows. But our Jack Russells were quite different. My daughter's dog was outstandingly cooperative, where as my dog, Cookie, should have been listed in the dictionary under the word *stubborn*. It was Cookie's efforts that did the most to reform my training methods away from the forceful techniques I learned up to that time.

I soon took on studies of dog training from books to seminars. I began to teach puppy classes, then agility, and even held a clinic or two. Soon, I had more and more people contacting me to help with their problematic dogs. Eventually, I quit my day job and took on training and writing full time. In 2002, I won my first award from the Dog Writers Association of America when I wrote about a problematic case I solved. I still study anything and everything I can about dog training and often study other trainer's techniques. Currently, I split my time between writing, consulting on problem dogs, and taking on project dogs from rescues. When I found the opportunity to write this book, I quickly realized that not only could I share my own personal experiences, but since I was so heavily networked with so many successful dog trainers, I could let them share what worked for their businesses.

Before You Begin

Becoming a dog trainer is a journey. What you will discover is that dog trainers are on an endless quest of learning while doing what they love. But to begin this journey, there are skills you will need. Because dog training is so diverse, in addition to some basic skills which are applicable to all dog training, you will also want to plan a course for what area you want to specialize in. But as you saw in chapter 1, sometimes even the best plotted journey can treat you to ideas you never imagined. One of the great things about the field of dog training is the opportunity to learn what others know and then build upon your own expertise.

Training, Skills, and Knowledge Needed

There are some valuable skills to hone no matter what area of dog training you choose. This kind of learning becomes a foundation for understanding dog behavior and training a dog. You also will find great value in becoming part of the dog community. So even if you are not yet a dog trainer, this is a good time to start networking with other dog people, and to become infused in the dog community. And last but not least, you need to rally your family support.

Chapter 12 talks more about the requirements for teaching different kinds of classes as well as certifications. However, long before you reach that point in your business, you need to have some preliminaries that support your dog expertise in the training business. Below are some areas you need to have or acquire to help you before you launch into a dog training business. These are skills that all dog trainers need.

Breed Education

Although it is true that no two dogs will necessarily act the same way in the same situation, certain breeds have behavior characteristics bred into them. For example, most retrieving breeds seem to naturally know what to do when you throw a ball. But toss that ball for a French Bull Dog, a breed developed as a companion, and most won't bother going after that ball. The differences in breeds of dogs can also require different techniques for successful or efficient training. Knowing the history and the development of different breeds can help you get into a dog's head as well as understand what drives different behaviors.

To help get a better understanding of dogs in general, people have categorized them. For example, many northern breeds often display characteristics closer to those of a wolf. On the other hand, companion breeds can lose enough of their predatory doggy roots that they probably couldn't even kill a mouse to survive in the wild. Other issues that drive behaviors we see in our dogs include high energy found in some working breeds, and higher chase drives. By understanding as many breeds as possible, from the dog's breed history though the breed traits, will help you better understand how best to train different dogs.

Although some of the best places to find information on different breeds of dogs can be reviewed online or in books, first-hand information is also critical. So work to get a higher education with different breeds. Go to different dog events such as agility, flyball, or other dog shows. A lot of times dog owners are just killing time waiting for their moment in the show ring. Since most people love to talk about their dogs, you can strike up a conversation and ask some questions about their specific breed. Some of the questions may include:

- Why did you choose this breed?
- How long have you owned this breed?
- What do you like about this breed?
- What do you find as a challenge with this breed?
- How easy were your dogs to train?
- What was the most difficult thing to teach your dog?
- What kinds of techniques did you find worked best?

Be cautious to weigh information that you get from any one person. One dog owner may have acquired a dog that is more compliant than the breed standard, and the owner isn't breed savvy enough to know that their poorer training techniques won't work with other dogs. To help gauge the advice you get from various individuals, watch those people when they show their dog and see how they work with their dogs. That will give you some insight as to the effectiveness of the techniques they've chosen. If you gather enough information from a variety of people on one particular breed, you may just discover things to try when you are training face-to-face with that breed.

The Different Developmental Stages of the Dog

A dog trainer needs to understand that puppies learn one way, adult dogs learn another way, and the transition from puppy to adult can be problematic for some dogs. Dogs also have other stages of development. Most dogs don't fully mature until they are three years of age, and up to that time can have age-related issues. If the dog is intact, that can change the behavior of the dog at different stages of development. Even senior dogs can take on a different role in a household as they age, especially in multi-dog households. To get a solid grasp of dog training and behavior, you need to educate yourself on how the different stages can affect a dog's learning and behavior.

Pack Behaviors

Many people equate wolf-pack behaviors to dog-pack behaviors. Although studying wolf packs can give some insights into certain dog behaviors, that study only scratches the surface. Dogs show social behaviors that can sometimes incorporate humans as part of a pack (wolves won't do this). Other factors that affect dog pack behaviors are numbers. In a two-dog household, especially with one owner, you fall far short of having enough individuals to fill the different roles of a pack. A household with an incomplete pack can affect dog behavior. Other factors in the environment can shape pack behaviors such as resource availability and space availability, or the lack of it. Canine personality and breed characteristics can also influence pack-like behaviors. Some breeds don't show much pack behavior at all. Even though a lot of factors can prevent normal pack interactions, understanding pack behaviors can also help when working with behavior issues.

Housetraining and Crate Training

Housetraining dogs and problems with housetraining dogs are often a big issue for a lot of dog owners and therefore often brought to dog trainers for resolution.

Even if you decide to specialize in specific areas of dog training, such as competition obedience, people with dog moxie are expected to understand how to resolve housetraining issues or, in the least, understand how to more easily housetrain a dog. Crate training, which goes hand in hand with most housetraining techniques, is also a must-know. But don't stop at the basics. If you plan on working with the average dog owner, you will be best served by learning how to deal with housetraining issues such as marking in the house, submissive peeing, and dogs who seem to elude success through typical housetraining attempts.

Canine Body Language

Dogs may bark for a variety of reasons, but when a dog really wants to communicate, a dog does that through body language. Oftentimes this language may seem subtle to the untrained eye, but to an experienced dog trainer, the information practically shouts a dog's intention. Although some expressions can be unique to a specific dog, a lot of the body language has universal meaning. In the least, you need to study canine body language enough to know that a dog will wag its tail both when happy and when tense enough to bite. Once you get the basics by pouring over books and videos, make sure you get as much field experience as possible in this area.

Canine Health, Nutrition, and Medicine (Both Traditional and Alternative)

Dog behavior issues and medical issues at times can go hand in hand. Although no dog trainer has the right to diagnose as if they were a veterinarian, a dog trainer needs to know and understand certain canine issues, especially those that can result in changes in dog behaviors. One common disease that can adversely affect a dog's behaviors is hypothyroidism. So study the basics and don't hesitate to have someone check with their veterinarian if you suspect a biological driving agent.

Teaching, Counseling, and People Skills

Since dog training demands you work with clients, you need to not only hone your dog training skills, you need to learn some good people skills as well. Some of those skills include learning good ways to interact with people and keeping your input positive, just like you do when dog training. Ironically, just as different breeds of dogs can benefit from different approaches when training, different base personalities in people may need different approaches when working with clients. In the least, you will need to learn how to work around people who become defensive about their dog's issues. You may even need to use some counseling skills to help people who are fighting the best path to take for the benefit of their dog.

Teaching is another area where you may want to do some learning. Although some people seem to have a knack for teaching, how to effectively teach can be taught. There are books and classes that can help train you in this area, should this be a weakness. But don't conclude your education with book learning. While studying trainers who are training dogs, you may want to also study how they teach people to train dogs. If you hear of a dog trainer who has exceptional people skills in your area, it may serve you well to see if you can volunteer as an assistant or find another way to mentor under that person.

Learn How to Run Your Business

Your dog training is a business. That means there are basic business skills you need to acquire to run your business well. Without those skills, those dreams can fail. You will find this book touches on a lot of areas for the small-business skills you need. But don't hesitate to expand your skills. There are books on specific areas if you feel you need to improve some of your business skills. There are also classes. SCORE is an organization where retired business people volunteer help. Check out score.org to find a chapter in your area.

Your Support System—Everyone in the Family Ends Up Involved

A good support system can make or break a new business, and when it comes to a home-based business, family support will always be important. Since few dog trainers can handle a class alone, one of the best places to find help is often within the family. Things such as setting up equipment and even being a training assistant can often make a big difference in the quality of class you are able to conduct. Even if you have arranged for volunteers to help in your class, there will always be times when those people have issues arise and you'll need someone to turn to. So from the very beginning, even though this business is your baby, talk over possible areas where your family can assist you. Get a feel for how much your family members really want to be involved. Look at what their strengths are and if they have something unique they can bring to the business.

One dog trainer found a good way to have her husband help with her business. The dog trainer's husband did marathon running, so the trainer asked him if he was willing to take along clients' dogs that needed exercise and he said yes. What began as a little addition to the business, turned into a steady income. With a little coaching, the husband not only helped burn off excess energy in his canine escorts, he even learned how to reform some of the dogs leash aggression issues. Even if you have young children, they can help you when it comes to socializing dogs to children.

When Family Is Part of a Business, Relationships Change

I had a lot of family support for my dog endeavors especially during the time my two children were in high school to early college. One thing that I realized when working with family members, is that children change and so will your relationship with them. In fact, having your kids involved in your business, when done correctly, will actually help develop their maturity. You need to embrace your kids' involvement in your business, and divide responsibility as your children mature and are ready to take things on.

This happened with me and my daughter. I was approached by a Jack Russell Terrier club who wanted me to judge their agility classes. I'd learned back in my early horse training years that I didn't like judging. My daughter stepped forward and said she'd like to take that on. It was at that point I realized how much she'd matured, both with her canine education (my son never pursued dog showing, but did help haul equipment and do other tasks) and in her ability to take on this responsibility. I also realized she had the talent to judge and had to admit she'd done some study on her own. I helped facilitate her request to be the agility judge and things went well. The point is when you are working with your children in a business setting, you need to give them some of the same respect you would any employee. This may be a bit of a balancing act in that some of the home interactions will be more like regular parenting, where as the business relationships need to take on a bit different relationship. It is a good idea to never scold your children or reprimand them in front of customers when you are conducting your business, just as it is never a good idea to do this to any employee.

Friends Can Be Valuable Assistants

People often choose their friends because they have similar interests, so don't be surprised if you find you have friends you can call to help on occasion. Talk to each friend and ask them a few questions. Tell your friends that you are starting a business and could use some help from time to time. Ask if they'd have some interest and query them as to what kinds of things they'd like to do. Then, get a feel for how much they'd be willing to help. How much a person is willing to help can vary with individuals, and with how close of a friend the person is. I once had to set up some agility equipment in a park for an event I was hosting. Since I was tied up with logistics, my husband had to set things up. However, wrestling an A-Frame is a two-person job. My husband asked a friend from his work who gladly showed up to lend a hand. Although we wouldn't ask this individual to do this on a repeat basis, he was more than happy to come to our aid that day. Something to consider when you ask friends for help is to not ask for more than they are happy to give. And on that note, don't hesitate to trade help on mundane tasks they need to do in exchange for work that helps out your business. This kind of help can keep costs down when a business is in its infancy, allowing the business to grow strong more easily with less initial financial output.

Reaching Out to Others in the Dog Community

Dog people become like a family. As with a family, you will need to learn quickly how not to squabble with those who you don't care for, and how to build strong relationships with others. In this unique family-like relationship, you will find that you can gather people around you who you respect and can draw on for knowledge. I have a call list of several "dog" people I contact if I run across a training issue that has me stumped. Sometimes these people have dealt with similar issues and have the answer I need. Other times they can point me in the direction of resources that can help me find my solution. Once in a while, after talking over the situation with another dog trainer, I figure out a solution which had before eluded me. In the least, I typically come away with some new things to try when solving the real tough issues.

The Importance of Networking

One of the best ways to find dog people who have a wealth of information and can sometimes help out your business is networking. Networking is the process of creating a support system of sharing information and services among individuals and groups with a common interest. Some of the best places to network include dog clubs, dog shows, dog events, and by associating with other dog trainers. To really be able to network in these environments, you need to strike up conversations with people. At a dog club, you may have the advantage of attending a social gathering or perhaps you can help out at shows the dog club sponsors. Helping at shows and events can put you in more direct contact with people who are often more dog savvy. You may even have the privilege of meeting a judge. One time while volunteering, I was able to talk candidly to a judge about the obedience competitors and what criteria she used for judging. The information was golden.

Don't count out networking with competitors. In between their classes, you'll find them hanging out in a chair or milling around. You can ask them how they got into dog showing, and decide if they're knowledgeable. If you feel good about your communications, you might want to take contact information if you feel this person is a possible resource in the future. Don't hesitate during the conversation to talk modestly about yourself and give out a business card. Other dog trainers are often found at dog events and dog shows. Keep on the look out for these people. If you liked the way they showed their dog, use that as a conversation opener. Remember, dog people love to talk about dogs. Also remember to give them time to talk so you can learn more about them, rather than you monopolizing the conversation by talking about yourself.

Thoughts About Networking on Online Forums

Dog forums are everywhere these days. Do a search and you can find a forum for every breed from a Jack Russell Terrier to a golden retriever. Most of these forums offer some area to post dog training issues. In addition to breed-specific

Janice Dearth Uses Online Forums Effectively

Janice is a trainer who shows dogs, and is an obedience and Rally judge. When she has issues or questions she wants input on, she often networks through a forum. But she doesn't just post anywhere. There are just too many forums that are poorly moderated or not moderated at all, and when she needs answers, she wants the best from the best. For that reason, she uses the Yahoo-based forum for the National Association of Obedience Instructors (NAOI). There she gets quality answers. Janice will acknowledge that the human factor can lead to disagreements on any forum, and some of those disagreements can take on a life of their own, but this forum has moderators to council or prevent some people from getting too far out of line in their responses. Janice serves as one of those moderators who reviews posts from people who have issues. Posts are routed to Janice and other moderators to ensure that the integrity of the forum is not compromised.

forums, there are forums available to post any and all kinds of dog questions no matter what the breed. Some of these forums have knowledgeable moderators who work hard to eliminate erroneous or inaccurate posts, but others leave posting options open.

If you decide to network for information with online forums, be very selective. These can become a source of incorrect information very quickly. Look for forums that show some kind of a knowledgeable person as a moderator. Keep in mind that a moderator's bias can become infused in the information that is posted. Perhaps the best kinds of forums are the ones with input from professionals who choose to share training information online.

Networking in Person

With Facebook, Twitter, and a host of online forums where you can meet other dog trainers and other people, you might wonder, why deal with real people? The easy answer is because you will deal with people when teaching classes or working with canine behavior issues. Even if you take a dog into your home for reform, at some point you need to deal with teaching the owner how to handle the reformed dog. Another reason to network in person is that although networking online or with a phone call can help you communicate over vast distances, there is a lot of value in networking one-on-one. In-person networking helps build your image in your local dog community. Typically people will make more of an effort to help someone they know personally over someone they've never met.

If You Need the Ideal Network of a Dog Trainer, Consider Creating Your Own

Sue Brown, owner of Love My Dog Training, was interested in starting a network long before she got the opportunity. She was the state representative in Colorado for ADPT. She made the effort to send out a greeting and stated she was willing to talk or chat with them. One of the people Sue met though her outreach program was Mindy Jarvis. Sue told her about her desire to start a network and Mindy was on board. They got together and laid out criteria for membership. They decided to follow the ADPT philosophy to be all inclusive; they would allow trainers and people looking to become trainers to join, as well as not restrict membership to people by training methods. Membership in ADPT was not required. They called their new group Colorado Dog Trainer's Network.

Today, the meetings for the network are held quarterly and run about three hours. Sue always arranges for one or two guest speakers to share their training experiences or to help educate others on the business aspects of being a dog trainer. The summer meeting is expanded to an entire day to allow clinics and interactive training events. Meeting not only allows for furthering training education, but allows for getting to know other trainers in person as well as informal chatting and networking with like-minded people.

To set up her network online, Sue chose Ning.com. Although using this networking system was free at first, there is now an annual charge for the service. She decided to stay with Ning.com despite the fee because places like Yahoo! didn't allow for fellow members to post their profile and link to their websites as readily. Sue feels the online networking has several advantages in that it allows the membership to be expanded to more remote areas in the state. People who can't travel to Denver are invited to follow the meeting online. The online networking between the quarterly meetings allows people to get to know each other better. It also makes it possible for people who live in remote areas to form mini-groups with nearby trainers. The online part of the network allows members to post questions online if they need to reach out for unique solutions to a training problem in between meetings. Another advantage of having the Colorado Dog Trainers Network is that clients who ask for a trainer in Colorado can receive a referral. If someone approaches either Sue or Mindy, or any of the other members with a dog issue, and if these people live outside of their travel area, they will refer them to other trainers. This group started out with twelve members, and now after three years, has 129 members. Colorado Dog Trainer's Network has been a very successful, educational, and supportive outlet for Colorado Trainers, as well as place to really get to know each other.

Building Your Name in the Dog Community

A lot of the suggestions made thus far to help build your business, to network, and even hone your skills work toward building your name in the dog community. From the very moment you begin the process of joining the dog community, you want people to speak well of you and your actions. So keep in mind that you need to, at all times, conduct yourself as a professional. Be courteous to people, even if they are not that way to you. Don't hesitate to lend a hand to a fellow dog person who needs one. Be sure to get out and go to dog events that complement your business. Join dog clubs that promote the kinds of training you are doing. During social events you may be wise to refrain from drinking alcohol. Don't make an issue about not drinking, just offer a polite "no thanks" if someone encourages you to drink. Keep in mind that people typically harbor a bit more respect for people who are not carefree and drinking, and that little bit of respect can go a long way in your future.

Avoiding Negative Dog Politics

It is easy to pick at faults of others. Ironically, just like our dogs, we don't respect weakness and sometimes people will verbally attack other's faults. Don't get involved. If you are in a group of people who are running down another dog person, the best thing to say is nothing. If the group continues to run down people, find a polite way to leave. Don't agree with them and don't disagree with them. Many a dog club has broken apart due to negative politics. Even if you are a member of a club in turmoil, keep your comments and negative feeling to yourself. In the long run, you will find that you retain more good contacts and are able to mine the good information people have by not joining in with the negativity.

How One Dog Professional Avoids Bad Politics

Linda Bollinger has worked in several different areas of dog business over the last forty years, including pet shop assistant manager, licensed Greyhound trainer, working hunting terriers, competitor, breeder, prominent in the dog magazine publishing world, and owner of her own grooming business. She understands the ins and outs of good politics and tact when dealing with dog people and dog clients.

Linda will tell you that she doesn't always agree with what some people may say, but when she does disagree, she works to do so with diplomacy: "You need to watch and listen. Look for an invitation for your opinion. The more adamant someone is about their opinion, if what you want to say is important the more nimble you need to be. A good approach is to acknowledge the other person's position before offering your own. If the person is really touchy, be very cautious. What will help you is to learn how to be assertive without being aggressive."

Mining Future Business—
Treating All Dog Contacts as Potential Customers

The world is full of people who own dogs. A lot of places you go you will see dogs with their people, and you will see signs of reverence for their dogs. Don't hesitate to ask people about their dogs and if you feel one of your classes can help someone, don't hesitate to politely mention what services you can provide. Although no one likes a hard-core salesperson, polite comments or useful information, without insisting the person run to your website and sign up, are typically met amiably.

Go to dog events in your area. In my area, one of the shopping centers hosts what they call "Bark at Briargate." At this event a variety of trainers, rescue organizations, and pet suppliers set up booths. It is a great place to meet others in the dog community and to talk with them. Other dog events in our area include Halloween contests, walks to raise money for rescues, canine dog charity events, and doggy events hosted in a park. Don't forget that dog shows also offer an opportunity to meet people. At some shows you may want to set up a booth, while at other shows you will simply want to mill around looking for opportunities to meet other dog people. Be aware that some of the other people milling around may be looking into things to do with their dogs and not actively participating in whatever show event is underway. These people may become your future clients.

Operating a home-based business allows you to be a little more relaxed than if you went to a brick-and-mortar establishment to work. After all, as the boss, you set the dress code. And when you are at home, who is to stop you from showing up in the early morning to do your paperwork dressed in your pajamas? Although you do have the comforts of home outside your office area, you still have the responsibilities of running your business as professionally as someone who rents a building and drives to a separate location. Don't be tempted to ignore the rules and regulations that accompany running a business out of your home. Instead, take the time to structure your business from the beginning so you will be in a good position to succeed and grow.

Setting Up Your Home Office Area

You can't casually operate a home-based business with success. You need to take on your business with the same responsibility people who run major businesses use. One way to get your business started on a professional basis is to do a good job setting up your home office area. Even the IRS recognizes that fact and they have specific regulations for how you set up your working area if you intend to use that area as a tax deduction. Some of their regulations, such as the requirement that this office space is a place to meet or deal with patients, clients, or customers in the normal course of their business, or in connection with their trade or business, or certain storage use such as inventory or product samples, are actually good concepts for you to consider when you set up your home office area. But before you embark on setting up your home office, here are a few questions to ask yourself:

- Is this an area where I can have enough privacy to conduct my business?
- Is there telephone access in this area?
- Is there good lighting, or can I upgrade the area for good lighting?
- Is there ample room for my computer, phone, office supplies, and other supplies I will need to have readily available?
- Is there additional equipment I need for my business and can that be stored in this area, or do I need a storage space in addition to my home office area?

Do You Really Need a Home Office?

Perhaps you plan on training as a consultant who visits people's homes, and armed with a cell phone you may ask if you really need a home office area. The answer is yes. Even if you handle your training classes at another facility, you need some kind of office area. A home office allows you more ability to handle client calls and keep track of paperwork. The following are things a home office helps you do well over just trying to wing it with a cell phone. A home office:

- Provides you with a private area for lengthy phone conversations.
- Gives you a place to organize your paperwork so you can easily access client information.
- Facilitates accounting tasks.
- Helps keep your business in order and your schedules well organized.
- Gives you a place to keep your business papers and any licenses.
- Provides an area for filing client information.
- Gives you a place to collect information that supports your business such as books and videos.

Another consideration to having a home office over merely fielding calls with a cell phone is that you need a permanent address for a lot of your business and forms as well as loan applications. Having a home office also allows you the convenience of receiving deliveries at your home.

Things You'll Need in Your Home Office

Computer

More and more we are able to access data from anywhere we happen to travel between smartphones and iPads. However, having a computer in your office is still a must. Whether you have a laptop or desktop, you need to have somewhere at home to help organize your information, coordinate your marketing efforts both online and offline, as well as keep in touch. At this time, most mobile devices don't have a high storage capacity. Although the future may change that, a desktop (or laptop) is a good investment. Another issue is that some of the smartphones are considered higher risk as far as security, more so than computers, when it comes to financial transactions. Although you can access the world via smartphones and iPads, doing a lot of work on these devices is not all that practical.

Fax and Printer

A printer is a must. If you are teaching classes, you will most likely be handing out a class syllabus and may hand out notes. You will also be printing out requirements for the class, refund policy, and a waiver for your students to sign. There are numerous other needs for a printer in your business. Even if you download a business form from the Internet, you often need to print it to fill it out and mail the form back. Although directions to a client's house may arrive by e-mail, you may need a printout along when following the directions to their house. Since some clients may e-mail you information on dog issues or even how to get to their house, printed material is still a necessary part of our lives.

The ability to fax material is needed from time to time. To keep down costs, you can often purchase a fax and printer combination that is often available at a relatively low cost. Another option is to scan and e-mail a lot of the material people once faxed. Fortunately, finding one machine to do all isn't that difficult. If you are planning on printing out a lot of material to hand out, you may want to check into buying a laser printer over an inkjet. Although color is fun, it isn't necessary and can prove costly. When selecting your printer, pay attention to the cost of the ink cartridges. Buying a low-cost printer is no deal if the ink cartridges cost too much. Don't just use price to guide your purchase. Make a list of the functions you need. I was able to find a printer that is also a scanner, fax, and copier. Instead of having two or three space-devouring devices, I have them all contained in one and the price was very reasonable. But before I bought this piece of office equipment, I went online to see if this worked well for the majority of users. Anytime you are investing in equipment, I'd recommend you do an Internet search to see if other customers are satisfied.

Filing Cabinet

Certainly, more and more the world is turning to e-mail for correspondences, and electronic correspondences are great. After all, they often help save a tree. Many e-mail hosts have a structure for allowing you to save your e-mails into electronic files. I use Google mail (gmail) and have several categories that allow me to keep track of electronic records I get via e-mail. But I still have some papers I need to keep track of, including my insurance policies. And files are still the best way to keep that paperwork organized. Although you may not have the need for a large cabinet, you will need a filing cabinet or a file box. If you don't feel you need a larger file cabinet, look into boxes that accommodate hanging file folders and can be kept out of the way in a corner, yet still be easy to access.

Book and DVD Storage

Since being a dog trainer is a lifelong learning experience, you will find yourself collecting books and some DVDs. Your home office is a great place to have a bookshelf to keep those books and DVDs in order to easily refer back to. Don't try and organize this as an afterthought. When you set up your home office, make the space and put them in a place where you can easily organize and access them.

Small Storage

The traditional office often had a large, heavy desk with a lot of drawers. Many people these days house their computer on a table or smaller desktop. Fortunately, there are small storage units, often made of plastic materials, that can accommodate miscellaneous office items from paperclips to pens. These organizational drawer systems can also allow you to have a place to keep things you need to find on a regular basis, such as your checkbook.

Phone

Perhaps you are considering operating with a cellphone only, and not having a landline. For some people, they can work out the logistics. But when you are teaching, you will not want to have the phone ringing for regular customers so this may leave you having to turn the phone on and off. If you are like me, when I get busy after a class finishes up, I too often forget to turn on my cell phone. For that reason, I prefer to have a landline for most of my business calls, and use the cell phone for contact when I am out of the office.

If you decide to have a landline for your business, you have some options. You can have a separate line for your business that will have a separate phone number. Unfortunately, this is more expensive than trying to use your home number as your business number. Another option, if your phone company will allow it, is to have a second phone number that rings on the same line as your main number. This "rider line number" will ring with a different tone. Many businesses use this kind of line as a fax line. However, you can also use the number as a business number that will be different from your home number. When clients call, the different ringtone will alert you that the call is for your business. The different tone can also tell your family that this is a business call, and if you aren't home, they can let the caller leave a message. That keeps those little pieces of paper that someone jots messages on from being an issue since those papers too often seem to get lost.

I use a rider line and like having a different number for my business. For me this helps out since when a phone call comes into my home, I need to gather my state of mind before engaging in a conversation. Let's face it, you can get a phone call any time day or night. Since I field a lot of calls from all over the United States, there have been times I've gotten calls at 5 a.m. Since I'm not a morning person, it helps for me to hear that different ringtone, so I can mentally prepare myself for talking to someone about dog issues. Other times, such as when I'm watching television, especially a comedy, I need to change my mindset for customers, whereas with many of my personal calls, that doesn't matter as much. No additional wiring is needed to add this feature, and phone companies often offer it for only a small fee, compared to a separate phone line.

Another feature to consider with a home office where you have a landline is your answering machine. If you use the rider line I talked about, you will not be able to set up a separate business answering machine for times you are not available to answer the phone. You can leave a message on your home answering machine that announces this number is for both a residence and a business. That message may be something like, "Hello, you have reached the 'your name' residence. Messages are also received for 'your business name.' Please leave your message after the beep. Thank you." Another option is to check with your phone company. Some phone companies offer an answering service as part of their service. If they do, see if they have a numeric identification for different message boxes. Services that offer this will have a greeting message followed by a statement similar to "To leave a message for 'your

dog business,' please press one. To leave a message for 'your residence' please press
two." Since you can often have three different message boxes, if you have children,
you can assign them one of the boxes.

Dog Area That Is Specific and Separate

Although your dog may lie at your feet in your office area while you attend to that
part of the business, the dog area that relates to your business will need to be specific
and separate. If you have a home where you can hold classes at your residence, your
dog area will probably be a small building outside your home, a garage, or an open
area in your backyard. If this is your intention, you need to make sure zoning and convenances allow for this kind of activity. Most trainers holding classes will probably be
using a facility outside their home (details on how to set up for that kind of training
facility are covered in more detail in chapter 10).

If you have a larger office, you may be able to keep an inventory of dog supplies
used in your classes or supplies you keep on hand to sell to customers. If not, find
an area where you can store these supplies. Since some of those supplies may be
dog treats, be sure to have an area that rodents can't easily access. Wherever you
choose to keep your supplies, be sure to make this an area where children or other
family members don't have a reason to come in, possibly moving things around or
disorganizing your material. By creating a separate area that doesn't have other
items your household needs to access, you can better keep your materials in order
and good working condition.

Convenances and Zoning

There are several layers of restrictions that can govern a home business. So begin your investigation of your residence from the regulations that are the most specific to your residence, and then work outward to be sure that you can operate a business there.

One of the first things to check is your housing development convenances. Although not all areas have convenances, some housing developments do. A restrictive convenance differs in the United States from a zoning regulation in that its creation and enforcement is a matter of contract between the landowners whose properties are affected by it, rather than an exercise of the governmental police power. Convenances, which are guidelines for how the neighborhood will conduct itself, can regulate certain behaviors in the neighborhood. The regulation of policies falls on your neighbors. For most areas with convenance, homeowner's associations are formed to do the enforcement. The homeowner's association will at times collect dues. The association will also be in charge of making sure convenances are followed. Those convenances can regulate everything from what color you can paint your house to operating a home business.

To find out if the area you live in has active convenances, begin your search with local real estate offices. A realtor can often look up convenances for different areas. If you do have convenances, get a copy and read through them. You can also check with your county zoning office. If you have any questions or concerns, contact the homeowner's association to find out if your business operation can proceed without any objections from your neighbors for convenance violations. Even though convenances are enforced by homeowner's associations, which are very often made up of homeowners in the area, don't write them off as unimportant. Homeowner's associations can and have taken individuals to court to enforce convenances.

Zoning is the practice of designating permitted uses of land based on mapped zones which separate one set of land uses from another. This concept of dictating the use of various areas for particular purposes in many cities began in ancient times. Zoning is commonly controlled by local governments such as counties and municipalities or may be limited by the state or even the national government.

Once you find you are in good shape as far as any convenances, you will need to check with your county zoning for any regulations, permits, fees, or restrictions concerning your home-based business. Often the county office can help clue you in about any state regulations or permits required. Don't forget to ask about any town or city regulations should you be located within a town or city limit.

Licensing and Permits

Certifications deal with an acknowledgment of your ability given by an organization or institution. Although dog trainers don't need certification in most states to call themselves a dog trainer, be sure to check the state where you live. More often, a state will have license requirements. More is discussed in chapter 12 on certifications. Licenses and permits deal with a government agency registering you to ensure you meet their legal requirements. Be sure to check with your state and, to be safe, ask them if your county and city have regulations. It is better to be safe than shut down.

Health Department and State Regulations

Many of the health department regulations are driven by states rather than counties and cities, but be sure to check with all that apply to your business. When working to see what the health regulations are, you may want to think ahead. Some dog trainers will take on training a dog for a week at their house. What that means is that you are kenneling the dog while doing one-on-one training. For some dogs, this training can really make a difference in changing a dog's unwanted behaviors; however, if this is a consideration on your part, make sure you check to see what restrictions apply. Some municipalities will not require special permits or health department inspection if one dog at a time is involved; however, if this is something you might pursue, do your homework before the need arises. If you live in an area that allows kenneling of dogs, you might find it advantageous to do the paperwork to operate a limited kennel. This will allow you to take on dogs from clients for more focused training, or to add to your income if a client feels more comfortable with you watching their dog when they are out of town.

Being a Good Neighbor

Even with a home-based dog training business, you may find you have two sets of neighbors. The first are those around your primary residence. If you have people coming to your home for training, be sure to tell them where they can and can't park so as to not intrude on your neighbors. Be sure to remind them to pick up any messes their dog makes and tell them to keep their dog leashed at all times. If your client has a hard time controlling their dog, make arrangements to meet them when they arrive and escort the dog from their vehicle to your home. Work hard to keep any barking to a minimum.

If your business requires you to go to a facility to train dogs, then make sure you also inform people about where their dogs can relieve themselves and how to pick up after their dogs. Take the time to police your clients and if you see any messes around the area, clean them up. Also make sure your clients know where they can and can't park. Talk to the other business owners in the area and invite them to come to you if there are any issues that arise. It is far better to set up an atmosphere of cooperation with your neighbors rather than finding yourself reacting to complaints.

04

Getting Down to Business

With the enthusiasm of a dog looking forward to that long-awaited walk, once you decide to start your business, it is tempting to charge out the door with unplanned energy. Although the idea of taking time to write a business plan may make you feel like you want to pull back on the leash and plant your feet, this one effort can make or break your business. Business plans help small business owners succeed, where the lack of one can cause either a failure or financial hardship that could have been avoided. A business plan allows you to focus your enthusiasm on the parts of your business you need to, as well as give you a structure to make sure you are on track for success. Below is information on the different areas of a business plan, from creating your mission statement through selecting your business name.

Your Business Plan

In your business plan, you will want to define the purpose of the business, who your target demographic is, state how you plan to market your business, look at what financials you have in place, where you will conduct your business, and what your hours of operation will be. All this planning can help you realize where your business fits in, since you may not be the only dog training operation in the area. Your business plan can also help you make plans for the future of your business.

There are several essential components of a small business plan, but there is no specific length. Content is key. Your business plan will become your roadmap that provides directions to plan your future and help avoid bumps in the road. By starting at the beginning and working your way through these items, you can better construct your plan.

Business Description

Write a convincing, short bio of who you are, your experience and expertise, and why customers or clients can benefit from your products or services. Include your name, address, and website. If you don't have a website, you will need to obtain one, and this is a good time to begin that task (see page 41). Describe what kind of training you plan to offer. Some things to consider might include if you are going to sell dog products. Evaluate the pros and cons of training that includes taking possession of the dog for a week or more at a time. Are you going to offer clinics now or in the future? Are you going to have structured classes, offer drop-in classes, or a combination of both? If you are doing dog behavior consultations, decide if you will even have clients bring the dog to your home for one-on-one consultations. If so, you will want to think about what kind of training equipment or facilities may help with problem dog behaviors. All of these components should figure in your business description. There is no predetermined length for your description. However, you will find that a thorough business description helps make sure you cover all your bases when it comes to other parts of your business such as adequate licenses and insurance.

Your Mission Statement

Some people may quickly write off their mission statement by summing it up as something simple like "to succeed and make money in my business." But take a moment to look at what a mission statement is all about. It is a statement of the purpose of a company, and it should guide the actions of the organization, spell out its overall goal, provide a sense of direction, and guide decision making. So even though you may casually say you want to make money as a trainer, your mission statement needs to say a lot more. Here are a few examples of what your statement may say: You plan on starting by teaching two classes a week and in a year, you hope to double that amount; you plan on teaching several kinds of classes, but eventually transition to behavioral consultations only; you hope in a few years to add employees, or plan on never adding employees; in two years you hope to be self-supporting enough to quit your day job and go into training full time.

Your mission statement will help you evaluate your current activities and help you know if you are on track for your current and long-term goals. To sum it all up, a well-done mission statement will begin with your dream and end with a plan that can succeed.

Short-Term and Long-Term Goals

In your business plan, you will have short-term and long-term goals. By sitting down and listing those goals as you work through your business plan, you can better work through some of the other financial information that will help when starting and running your business. One example of how a short-term goal can end up shaping some of the financial information you work with is the illustration for the six-month Cash Flow Statement on page 67. The income numbers for that table were not arrived at by throwing a dart at a dartboard with figures attached. This table is a good illustration of how a start-up business might proceed once you open your doors for business. Looking over the information in the table can help you understand the thought process of what goes into income expectations. In this example, the dog-business owner had done her homework. She knew that opening her doors in January would be a better time than doing so in November or December. So while a lot of her future clients were busy with the holidays, this business owner worked to set up for opening after the first of the year. Some of the money she spent in anticipation of that opening doesn't show up on the cash flow analysis. Expenses such as getting her website up and running and rent deposits were paid before she opened her doors. Her short-term goal was to teach four different kinds of classes with ten people per class. She planned on starting two different classes each month, instead of starting all four in the same month. Once they started, they'd run for eight weeks, meaning she'd again start that next class on a cycle that kept her beginning only two new classes each month. Her ideal class size was ten students. She planned on giving herself six months to reach the goal of teaching four classes at full capacity. Then, at the end of six months, she'd reevaluate to see if she could take on more classes by herself, if she'd need to hire someone, or if she planned on expanding classes. Although more information about doing a Cash Flow Projection is on page 66, you can glance at the table now to hopefully realize how some of the planning you are doing in your business plan plays out in your business success.

Marketing Plan

Even if you are the best darn dog trainer there is, you need customers to be successful. That means you need to communicate your services to potential customers. A marketing plan details how you plan to do it. That makes a marketing plan an important part of the business plan. The first step in coming up with a good marketing plan is to look carefully at the needs of your customer. Keep in mind that although you can clearly see the value of everyone taking both your puppy class and the class that follows, your public may not see that. They don't know that puppy socialization involves a key learning time in their dog's life, and can greatly shape the later behavior of the dog. Nor do they know that as their dog enters adolescence, it can better make the transition into a well-behaved adult dog by attending your well-crafted class. At times, with dog training, one of the keys is to educate the public not only about what services you have, but about how and why dog owners need these services, and how they and their dogs will benefit.

The good news is that nowadays there are a lot of dogs in many households. All you have to do is help dog owners understand how your services can fit their needs. But before you begin thinking up ideas, take a moment to look at the demographics of the dog population. If you are in an area where there are a larger number of pit bulls and Rottweilers in the population, you may work to reach out to those people with a class that fills a training need so these dogs don't end up with unwanted human or animal attacks. If your area has a lot of activity-oriented people who are often biking or running, you may want to tailor classes that appeal to that kind of demographic. So do a little research about the dog-owning population around you, and learn about what kinds of dogs they have and what kinds of problems they may encounter so you can create classes that are more in demand. Pay attention to gender and age when you do your research. If you have a larger, aging population, pay attention to what might suit their needs along the lines of dog training. Identify your competitors and determine what makes your small business stand out from the rest. Check and see what the average income is, especially if you can equate that to the dog-owning population. All of this can help you shape a more successful business, determine what kinds of training to offer, and if you should attempt to sell products along with your training services. Chapter 11 discusses in detail some of these marketing ideas. After you review that information, do your marketing research and plan your marketing strategies. You can then add marketing costs to your business plan.

Organizational and Management Plans

When you start a home-based business, you quickly find out the meaning of the expression "wearing several hats." One of those hats is management. A good manager is also a good delegator. There will be several aspects of your business that you will do yourself, and some that you will delegate to others. When constructing your business plan, this is a good time to think that part of the business through. For example, if you are conducting classes, will you need an assistant? Will you need people to help set up equipment? Or will you incorporate equipment setup as part of your class requirements for your students, those people who show up in your class eager to learn. Some demographics will go for that concept, but others may not. By thinking things through at this stage, you can be better prepared when it comes to moving forward once you get your business started.

Don't hesitate to be creative if you need specific help. Look for people who might want to trade work for lessons. Certain levels of agility, such as drop-in classes, may have participants who are willing to help in with rearranging equipment. However, some people will be resistant to this kind of idea. If you find your demographics won't go for moving equipment, you will need to make other arrangements. Don't leave this issue to be discovered after you begin classes. Now is the time to think about what your needs will be and how you will meet them. Do your thinking, and do some research as to how you will solve the logistics of running your business. Don't hesitate to observe how some of your competitors run their classes.

Financial Plan

This is a vital part of your business plan, especially if you may need potential investors or a small business loan as a start-up. Your financial plan will help you decide how quickly you can grow your business. You need to take a look at a one-year cash flow projection. Some of the tools to help you look at finances, such as balance sheet and profit and loss statements, are discussed in more detail in chapter 5. Some of the financials you need to consider when doing your business plan include any costs for running your classes, such as rent. Then, you need to estimate how many classes you need to have each week to pay the bills. One of the factors will be class size. By working through a business plan now, you will better be able to decide the smallest size class you can have before it becomes economically unfeasible. By sitting down and working through the numbers before you get started, you will better be able to prevent losing money before you realize things in the business need changing. Don't forget to include other costs such as lawyer fees, accounting fees, and other overhead, including gasoline for your vehicle. By using a balance sheet and expense worksheets, you can see at a glance what kinds of expenses you need to manage. In the balance sheets and other samples found in chapter 5, the information was exampled with the assumption that the small business owner took out a start-up loan. Some of the money from this loan was spent fairly quickly to get the business underway and to acquire equipment. Some of the money was kept in reserve. When doing your financial planning, keep in mind that for most businesses, it isn't unusual to take a year or two before the business can cover operating costs and even longer before the business makes a profit.

The Right Balance for Success

Daniel Will, an MBA from the University of Colorado, draws on his education and experience as a distribution channel manager at Agilent Technologies, Inc., to give some advice to start-up businesses. According to Daniel, small business owners can become insolvent (unable to pay their bills) if they get too aggressive during the infant stages of their business. There are two particular areas small business owners need to take caution. The first is in the estimate of the total addressable market opportunity. A common problem happens when the business owner doesn't properly estimate the total size of the market, and then segment it to focus their business strategy on the subset of customers who are going to want their unique service offering. A business owner must know the total addressable market in the locale they will service. They must then know what level of differentiated and/or discounted service they will be providing within that market that will attract the key set of clientele they are going after out of this total addressable market. Doing this properly will help the business owner identify what the potential mature level of income is that can be secured.

The second is the conservative estimate of the number of months the business owner expects it will take to ramp up to this mature level of income. An estimated increasing income by month is generated, starting at zero from when the business opens its doors. Having an estimate of the income by month from zero to maturity, the business owner should then conservatively develop an expense budget using the Income Statement (see chapter 5, page 63) as a tool. A successful business plan must ensure that monthly expenses scale increasing income to help ensure the business turns a profit by an expected point in time. Ideally, the business turns a profit in month one if business expenses are kept to an absolute minimum while income is small, and then increases accordingly as income increases. This is not always possible because an initial amount of expense is required to start a particular business. If this is the case, you will need to make an estimate of the amount of time it will take to pay back this initial cash or debt investment with business profits. Business owners can commonly get too optimistic when estimating the market opportunity coupled with incorrect expectations for how long it takes to get there. This puts the business in a position where it cannot pay its bills including any minimum debt payments and drives it into bankruptcy. The key is to pair your expenses with your income and do not get overly ambitious.

When business owners use debt as a financial instrument to get a small business initially started, they are that much more susceptible of not being able to pay their bills during those especially difficult start-up months. Inevitably what can also occur are macroeconomic conditions that cannot be forecasted, and a small business with little to no debt can more easily wade through these turbulent times. Having a conservatively generated expense budget paired with income that allows for some additional headroom is even that much more critical with debt involved. If you are fortunate enough to start your business using your own saved cash, you will be in a much better position to wade through the variety of uncertainties that may hit while your company is in an infant state. Even if not using debt to start your business, a conservatively generated budget paired with income is still important to help ensure your business can pay its monthly bills and remain solvent.

What's in a Name?

In 1999, Agilent Technologies decided to break away from Hewlett Packard to form its own entity. Hundreds of thousands of dollars were spent coming up with this name. Factors taken into consideration included international compatibility, any similar names this one would be confused with, legal implications and ramifications, and the community of customers for the business. When you look for your ideal name, although you may not be able to spend money to come up with a name, you need to consider some of the same issues and choose wisely. You want a name that communicates the kind of business you are, so make your name meaningful. Some people may have an ideal surname that can work well as part of their business name. If you don't have an easy-to-remember, pronounce, or understand name, you may pass on using it as part of your business name. Whatever name you choose, make sure this is one you can live with. One of my most educational, memorable, and all-round heart stealing dogs was named Cookie. This extremely challenging dog to me represents a great deal of training education I had to master to successfully train her. However, to the public, there wouldn't be the same association. For most people, the word *cookie* doesn't bring higher-level dog training skills to mind. Instead, when people associate the word *cookie* with dog training, they typically think of a dog treat. So when you look for a good name for your business, consider one which looks good in print, is unique, and has meaning to the public you are trying to reach.

Another must when choosing a name is to make sure that no other local business has the same name. The last thing you need is to find out that another established trainer has, or uses a name that can easily be confused with yours. Another factor is the frequency of similar names. In my area, the term K-9 is used in several forms by several training businesses. That similarity can make any one of them too easy to confuse with another and more difficult to stand out as the better choice. In general, if you are trying to sell yourself as an individual dog trainer your name alone may suffice. However, if you are trying to sell training classes as your primary business, work to include that information in your name. Consider using the word agility as part of your name if that is your only specialty, or the word training to make sure people can identify what your business offers. Try and find a name people will remember, and one that is more unique. Although you want catchy, stay away from anything that takes away from a more professional persona.

Your Logo and Business Image

We live in a media-saturated, visually stimulated world. All around us are images, sometimes flashing or strobing, working to gain our attention. That creates a tendency to block out a lot of this stimulus. However, almost all dog owners find themselves wanting to take a second look when they see a picture of a dog. A good logo as part of your business image can help you capture the attention of your potential clients. A good logo can make you identifiable at a glance, and when you use that logo consistently, can help build your image.

A logo helps you with your company image and can definitely help brand the company. Any graphics used in the logo need to be simple. Keep in mind that people expect information at a glance. Your message will be lost if your logo is too complicated or busy. Color template and fonts are important, and need to balance being eye-catching, but not distracting. Having a standardized font is also important from the standpoint that it provides consistency in the look. As well, choose a font that is readable when used in a variety of marketing media, including store sign, print media, flyers, business cards, etc. So if you don't already have a logo, consider using a logo to help identify your business. It can be just as valuable as your name. When choosing your logo, look around for examples with strong appeal. Take your time to construct two or three ideas, and don't hesitate to ask acquaintances what they feel works well. Remember your logo will become part of your image.

Obtaining a Website Address

These days, almost as important as picking the right name for your business is securing a website address. Let's face it: The Internet is replacing a lot of other ways for locating all kinds of information, including dog trainers. A web page can not only tell people how to get ahold of you, it can tell people all about your business and, if done well, just how your services can meet their needs. Since your website is closely tied to your name, as soon as you choose a business name, or perhaps simultaneously, you need to secure your website address.

There is terminology that goes along with becoming part of the World Wide Web. What you will need to obtain is known as a domain name and/or IP (Internet Protocol) address. For example, my domain name is peggyswager.com. If you do a Google or Internet Explorer search for Peggy Swager, my web page domain address will come up. Although my domain name is peggyswager.com, my actual website address is http://www.peggyswager.com. This full address is referred to as a URL, which stands for Uniform Resource Locator. This URL takes you to my home page. However, I have several other pages on my site that may interest people. Each of those pages has a slightly different URL, kind of like different chapters in a book. For example, to view the article that I won an award for on submissive peeing, you could type in the exact URL and go to that exact page, passing the home page. That URL is http://www.peggyswager.com/article_submissive.php. But most home pages make things a lot easier for people by allowing you to click on links that take you to different parts of the website. When you go to acquire your domain name, you only have to buy the main name, just like you only buy a total book, without having to pay any extra for the chapters contained within. Pages in a website are simply subsets of the main website.

When you buy your domain or website address—your home page name—this will not be a one-time purchase. There is an expense to every website name to make it work like it needs to. A website name will have tracking fees, looking-up fees, and fees to secure that no one else can use your website name in the entire world. So expect to pay a yearly fee for your name to whichever company you choose to register your name with.

Another yearly fee you will pay is a place to host your website. Hosting a website is done on a computer, but this is not a regular home computer project. There are software considerations and hardware requirements that make hosting your own website impractical. More importantly, website hosts will be responsible for providing a certain amount of security for your website. There is a lot of expense that goes into the processors that make websites work. This has resulted in several companies whose business it is to host websites.

The time to secure your domain name is right after you choose your business name. When you go to register your name with a company that offers that kind of service, they are set up to do a search for the name you want to use. As stated before, each domain name must be unique. So if you want to use the name caninesolutions .com, that one is not available. Since you can't use caninesolutions.com, you may need to modify your name. One example of how to do that is to register your URL as caninesolutionsLA.com, which can work if you are in the Los Angeles area.

The other side of the URL coin is that too similar of a name can cause people issues. Some people looking for your website may type in caninesolutions.com while others may type in caninesolution.com. A simple plural of a word creates a different website location. To help better accommodate people looking for your website, if it is possible, consider buying your main domain name and any very similar domain name that may be used by searchers. In this case, if you called yourself Canine Solutions, you'd buy both caninesolutions.com and caninesolution.com. By purchasing both the singular and the plural form of your name, both can easily be used, and more people will successfully reach your web page. Purchasing two URLs for your website doesn't mean you have to have two separate websites. Your website designer can create one website for your main URL, and then point your other URL to that same site. People typing in either URL will go to the same place and probably never know the difference.

Although I've given the examples of buying a .com name, there are numerous other extensions, including .org, .gov, .edu, .net, and more. Typically, a .org is used for non-profit organizations, and .gov for government, as well as other specifics for other extensions for other purposes. You are best served if you can secure a .com as this is the extension for commerce and most often used by businesses. People trying to find you on the web will expect to find you with a .com name.

Domain Names and Web Hosts

Years ago, when I first registered my URL for my domain name, I did it after searching the Internet and finding a very good value. Unfortunately, this company began to get a bad reputation and if you had any issues, you couldn't get ahold of them. So I switched to the company that had my web hosting, even though I was paying more per year. The customer support was worth the cost. A couple of take-away lessons from this are: You can change your domain name registry to a different company if you need to, and the cheapest may or may not be the best. Before you give them your charge card or credit card number to secure that domain name, do a search for complaints against the company. My first company had racked up a lot of complaints. The same may be true for your web-hosting company. But take that one step further. After you search for complaints, call up their customer service. If you find you can't readily get ahold of anyone in technical support, then pass on that company.

What Is an 'IP Address'?

You see this "IP address" expression more and more. Your computer has an IP address, your phone has an IP address. Even Coke machines have IP addresses. Cops on CSI and other TV shows trace criminals by their IP addresses. But what exactly is an IP address? An IP address, or Internet Protocol address, is a unique identifying number given to every single computer on the Internet. Like a car license plate, an IP address is a special serial number used for identification.

IP address is not the same as a www. domain name address. For nearly every web server, the IP address is invisibly translated into a natural English domain name for ease of use. But technically speaking, the IP address is the true identifier of a web server. The domain name is simply a redirector pointer to help people find the web server. Your public will want your domain name while your web host will want your IP address.

Business Structure Options

There are a host of options for you as a small business when it comes to how you structure that business. What you choose to become, whether a sole proprietor or an LLC, a partnership or an LLP, or even a corporation, you have two main considerations to weigh when making your decision: The first is that different business structures have different tax liabilities; the second is that different structures have different amounts of protection should someone decide to sue you. The most common kinds of structures for someone beginning a new business are sole proprietor, partnership, or LLC. Each of these functions differently and each has advantages and disadvantages. Below is a brief description of the different structures.

Sole Proprietor

A sole proprietorship is also known as a sole trader or simply a proprietorship. This kind of a business is owned by one individual, and that person will manage the business. As the owner of the business, you receive all profits (subject to taxation specific to the business) and have responsibility for all losses and debts. This means that the owner has no less liability, both tax and legally, than they would if they were acting as an individual instead of as a business. Although you can have a trade name, you can also simply use your legal name. You generally need to file a DBA (doing business as) statement with the local authorities (check your state regulations to be sure). If you are a sole proprietor, you will report your personal taxes on a Schedule C and use a Form 4562 for depreciation. You will also be paying self-employment taxes. Self-employment taxes consist of Social Security and Medicare. A sole proprietorship is the easiest structure for operations, but considered the most expensive as far as your tax structure. That being said, this still works well for people who are just beginning a business. You will find this system makes it easy to get at the money you've earned in your business as opposed to other kinds of structures. What this means is that if you want to take money out of your business for personal use, all you need to do is write a check. When it comes to liabilities with a sole proprietorship, this structure doesn't offer any extra protection.

Partnership

Perhaps you are not feeling bold enough to take on a business by yourself, or perhaps you and your dog training friend are thinking about starting a business, and since you have similar aspirations and enthusiasm, you both see the advantage of doing this adventure together. If you plan on beginning a business with another individual, you will do so by forming a partnership. But there are a lot of precautions you need to consider before taking on this kind of relationship in a business.

Although you and your prospective partner get along quite well now, a partnership can test any relationship. Your involvement level with your partner will far exceed the one you have now. For that reason, you need to be able to get along with a partner as you would in a healthy marriage. Businesses can struggle, and you and your partner will have to endure this struggle together, and like many marriages, problems often come down to money. This can create contention between two partners. One thing that can help people who are considering becoming partners is to sit down and talk through some of the issues that may arise. If you still feel that you and your partner are right for this kind of a relationship, you will be served well to put in writing the equivalent of a prenuptial.

When you sit down for the discussion phase, talk about what you see as the beginning goal, middle goal, and ending goal of the business. Partnerships are seldom conducted as if one individual now has half the work because of the partner. There is almost always one person who is the lead on the business. If you both see yourselves as the one in the lead, then you need to establish a way to come to decision on issues should the two of you have different ways to do things. You may also want to discuss who will do different aspects of the tasks needed to run the business. Keep in mind that you have the choice of financially splitting a partnership fifty-fifty, or you can have any other arrangement such as twenty-eighty. If you opt for an unequal split of your partnership, then you will probably have an uneven split when it comes to contributions or taxes.

If you decide to do a partnership, it is generally recommended that an agreement is written out spelling out the responsibilities that each partner carries. Some of the items you want to state in your partnership include: financial contributions of each partner; allocation of profits and losses; each partner's authority; management responsibilities; and what happens if one of the partners dies. As well, you may want to make provisions as to how disputes will be settled. If your finances are done evenly, and one person looks toward investing to expand, the other person needs to be willing to also commit capital.

On the subject of finances, just as the demise of many marriages can be traced to finances, partnerships can also have issues with money. That can lead to a split up of a partnership. You need to decide ahead of time should philosophies change and the partnership no longer works, how you two can go your separate ways. Since this will involve a buyout, you will need to get a lawyer to help construct the ground rules.

In a partnership you form a separate legal and tax entity. A partnership does give you some legal protections. Taxwise, when you get to the end of the year, you are going to do a separate tax return for the partnership. You file the partnership on a 1065. Then you get a K-1, used by a Partnership or S-Corporation to report a partner/shareholder's distributed share of income that represents your share of the profits. You take your share to your personal taxes. That part of your tax obligation will be taxed the same way as a sole proprietor. Your part of your income will be subject to self-employment taxes. Your tax lawyer and accountant are good consultants for helping to set up the best structure for your partnership and to help you decide if you should do an LLP (Limited Liability Partnership).

LLC

LLC stands for Limited Liability Company. For someone just starting out in business, they may not see any advantage in an LLC, especially if their goal is to remain a sole proprietor. But, there are several advantages to becoming an LLC for the sole proprietor. Those advantages often include some tax advantages, as well as liability advantages.

LLCs vary from state to state. Some people will find there are some tax advantages with their LLC, where others will not find any difference between a sole proprietorship and an LLC when it comes to taxes. You can consult with your accountant to check out if those advantages apply to your business.

Perhaps one of the biggest advantages to having an LLC over being a sole proprietor is that the LLC legally gives you more liability protection should someone sue you. Even if you begin as sole proprietors, you can easily transition into an LLC structure. You can often find the form to file online by searching under information for your state. Typically the cost of applying for an LLC is not a large one, nor are the annual fees excessive. Some people feel that the boilerplate LLC found online works well for them when registering their business. Others may want to consult with a lawyer or talk with their accountant before making a final decision.

S-Corporation

For most dog trainers, either an LLC or a sole proprietorship offers them just what they need for their business. But if you see an advantage in having a corporation, one to consider is the S-Corporation. Dog trainers who are more likely to choose this option are going to be larger companies with a solid income. Often, a business that has been well established may decide to move into an S-Corporation after the business has established a good track record of sustained income. But be aware that this kind of a corporation will not allow you some of the liberties you had with your sole proprietorship or your LLC. With the sole proprietorship or an LLC, if you want to take cash out of a business, you simply write a check. With an S-Corporation, you can't. In this business structure, your bookkeeping will be different. You will be paid from payroll, just like any other employee. Likewise, you will not have self-employment tax, but instead will have a deduction from your wages like a regular employee.

The S-Corporation has tax advantages for a company with more income. It also has advantages for liabilities. Although few start-up dog trainers will want to go this path to begin with, it can be a strong consideration once the company grows. So if you find you have enough income to make a regular payroll, or plan on expanding to take on a loan or a more permanent facility, this may be something to investigate.

Corporation

Corporations typically bring to mind big buildings with shiny glass windows. You will want to do a corporation when you need a lot of separation between you and your business. A corporation is a stand-alone operation. You won't have the freedom to move your money between your personal and your business account like you do a sole proprietorship or an LLC. Corporations typically are mired in a lot more paperwork and bookkeeping than a proprietorship, an LLC, or even an S-Corporation. Few dog trainers will ever end up with a corporation unless they undertake building a facility, and even then they have other options. Like the S-Corporation, a corporation does have more liability protection; however, for most dog trainers an LLC also offers liability and may be enough if you carry adequate insurance. If you wonder if a corporation is really right for you, you need to talk to your attorney and your accountant to better educate yourself about what are your best options. Keep in mind that you can't simply start with a corporation, then discover that it wasn't the best idea after all. Trying to change from corporation status to a sole proprietorship or LLC will carry huge tax obligations.

Why You Need an Attorney

These days with the Internet at hand, you might wonder if any question can't be answered with the click of a mouse. Even if you are quite skillful with your Internet searches, there will be times and issues where you will be well served by seeking professional advice. A good lawyer can help you with a decision and make sure your legal rights are protected.

Lawyers tend to specialize. Some only do estate planning, while others work with personal injuries. Business lawyers are professionals who have knowledge and experience with the starting and running of a business. Many lawyers also specialize in tax issues. Choose a lawyer who has small business experience, and preferably some experience with the dog training business or very similar types of service businesses. But before you dial the phone and find out how much these rather expensive professionals cost, price around. Some lawyers charge a lot more than others for the same service. It is also better to seek a recommendation. If you can't get a recommendation, then ask the prospective lawyer for some satisfied customers you can contact.

Before undertaking the cost of a lawyer, make sure what you want to deal with legally isn't something you can do for yourself. Things such as writing a business plan, researching and picking a business name, reserving a domain name for your website, applying for an employer identification number (EIN), which you will need for employee tax purposes, and applying for any licenses and permits the business requires are all things you can do yourself with a bit of Internet searching as your aid. If you don't feel as if you can handle government applications, you may want to see if your accountant or bookkeeper can help you apply for these since these professionals charge less per hour than a lawyer. If you are looking into doing a partnership agreement, or have some legal issues or uncertainties about doing a limited liability company (LLC), you may do well to consult a lawyer. Anytime you have complex business issues, a client who is threatening to sue, a complaint filed against you that you can't resolve yourself, a citation for a violation of any laws you can't resolve yourself, then consulting a lawyer makes sense. You may also want to employ a lawyer to help create a legal form for clients to sign which releases you of any liability concerning them or their dogs during classes or any training session.

05

Taxes and Record Keeping

Record keeping, more often called bookkeeping, is a necessary part of any small business. The information you gather has many functions. Reports generated from your income and expenses can tell you the overall health of your business or help point out problematic areas. The tabulation of your accounts will generate information for paying your taxes. And a profit and loss statement, as well as a balance sheet, will be required should you seek outside financing. Whether you act as your own bookkeeper or hire that service out, you need to understand the basics of taxes and record keeping.

The Difference between Bookkeeping and Accounting

Sometimes the terms bookkeeping and accounting are used loosely. In many cases it doesn't matter how you use the words, but if you want to be technically correct, you need to look at what job is being performed. Bookkeeping is simply the recording of the financials of the business. Bookkeepers keep the books, or record transactions for a company. Some of their duties may also include doing payroll. Bookkeepers can also prepare financial statements.

Accounting is more often the manipulation of that information. Accountants are the people who set up the accounts used by the bookkeepers. They also monitor and interpret the information generated by bookkeeping. Accountants need to understand the bookkeeping process and may supervise a bookkeeper. Some states regulate the title of accountant, giving you a better guarantee of the schooling these people have when it comes to laws and regulations.

Doing Bookkeeping Yourself or Hiring It Out

Too often, people who have never done bookkeeping cringe when it comes to the idea of taxes, forms, and record keeping. Perhaps part of the issue is that in this area, too many people starting up their business are not sure what all is involved and just where to start. Some may hope just to hire an accountant and figure that the accountant can make all the information work out right. Perhaps because I worked doing bookkeeping for several small businesses and one larger business during my college years, I don't harbor a lot of fear about the bookkeeping needed for a small business. However, during those years of working as a bookkeeper for other small businesses, I learned some very important lessons, including that you can't blindly let someone else take charge of your finances, without having a good idea of what's going on in the accounting department. Two businesses I worked for had some severe accounting errors I discovered after going to work for them. The owners had simply put trust in either a bookkeeper or an accountant without understanding anything about their business records. Both these businesses had errors totaling over ten thousand dollars, and one ended up refiling taxes from the previous year as a result of poor bookkeeping. That refiling of taxes resulted in the company being audited by the IRS. The moral of the story is that even if you decide to hire out all the bookkeeping, accounting, and taxes to other professionals, you need to learn enough about what is going on that you can look over the figures on a regular basis to be sure your expectations of the finances match what is being posted to the books. If you do decide to have someone else do your bookkeeping, be sure to get several references from happy customers. Sometimes your accountant can recommend a good bookkeeper, or may provide that service in addition to accounting. If you hire a bookkeeper, sit down on a monthly basis and look over the records. If your book-keeper can't explain your accounts to your satisfaction, then you need to look for a different bookkeeper.

Factors to Consider Before Taking on Bookkeeping and Accounting

When you run your own business, you need to have a lot of talent in several areas, not just dog training. You also need to know what to hire out and what is reasonable to take on yourself. The bookkeeping, accounting issues, and doing taxes are all areas that have the option of hiring out. But that can quickly become expensive. Ideally, a good business manager learns what he or she can do for themselves, and when it is best to hire a professional. Perhaps I have a bias because I learned bookkeeping in college, but I feel that for most people, it is reasonable to learn how to keep their own books. However, the accounting issues take more expertise and a lot of time because accountants need to keep up on current tax issues. With few exceptions, it is better to hire an accountant to do your taxes and to council you on organizing your bookkeeping. If you do decide to take on your own bookkeeping, expect to work under your accountant's guidance at first until you learn the ropes. If you decide not to try bookkeeping, be sure to learn enough about what all is going on so you don't end up with costly bookkeeping errors, because you are responsible for your bookkeeping accuracy, even if you are not doing the books.

How to Choose an Accountant

When looking for an accountant, you should check to see what credentials the person has. See if he or she is merely someone who has worked in that capacity in a business, if he or she has completed schooling, or if he or she is a CPA (Certified Public Accountant). Be aware that regulations for people to call themselves an accountant can vary state by state.

Before Looking for Your Accountant

Before looking for an accountant, it is a good idea to get a clear idea what an accountant does and doesn't do. As mentioned before, this individual can monitor and interpret information. For this reason, good accountants can also give some valuable business advice. If you don't need an accountant to help understand your financials, you probably will need one to help do your taxes. Tax codes are constantly changing. Learning them, understanding them, and keeping abreast of the changes is more than a full-time job. You will not have time to do this adequately and run your business. Therefore, hiring an accountant for most people is a necessity. If you decide to take on your own bookkeeping you will find a good accountant can sometimes help you learn the bookkeeping you need to manage your own office work and they can be very helpful in setting up categories for posting (what you call recording of the money you take in and spend). Accountants can often help you file for government forms if you are having a hard time understanding the process or interpreting government lingo.

Let the Search Begin

One good way to find an accountant is to get a recommendation. Check with others who are already in the dog business. Having an accountant who is familiar with the dog business or, in the least, familiar with similar smaller businesses will end up working out better for your business. There are several smaller items unique to every business, and the more familiar your accountant is with your business, the more likely your accounting will be done accurately. Even the best accountants make mistakes, and when they do, you end up paying for that mistake. So search for an accountant who is more likely to know more details about your specific business and better be able to help you accurately set up your bookkeeping. Once you find someone you feel may work as your accountant, do an interview with them. A few questions to ask may include:

- How long have you been in this business?
- Are you a member of an association?
- Are you a CPA?
- What is your Preparer Tax Identification Number? New regulations require all paid preparers, including CPAs and attorneys, to apply for a PTIN before preparing any federal tax returns beginning in 2011. If your accountant isn't up on that, then you should worry about her keeping up on other accounting issues.
- Have you in the past or are you currently doing accounts for a dog training business? If the answer is no, then ask if she or he has done similar businesses, then have her tell you how this business is similar.
- What is the fee? Some accountants may charge a single fee at the end of the year to do your taxes, but allow you to call up with simple questions during the year without an extra charge. Other accountants may charge an hourly fee for any over the phone advice. If what you ask takes research, then are you willing to pay an additional fee, but for short questions the accountant in question should already know, clients prefer free answers.
- Ask for three references to contact. Too often, people make the mistake when they are given three references of only calling the first one. After a satisfactory report, they don't check the other two references. Often, references are given in the order that a person expects to get good reports. So if you are tempted to skimp on calling all three references, then skip the first and contact the second one. If you get a good report, then contact the third one. If you are getting mixed signals, you may want to take the time to call the first reference, or ask additional questions to better investigate your uncertainties.

Accounting—Big versus Small Firms

Shanna Clark, a bookkeeper, and her husband, Bryan, a CPA, have worked in both larger corporations in various fields, as well as smaller firms giving them both a broad base of experience. Shanna now co-owns Clark Accounting Service, LLC with her husband, a firm that specializes in smaller businesses. She shares some observations about larger firms versus smaller accounting firms.

According to Shanna, all CPAs, big or small, are required to maintain their licenses with continuing education. One thing Shanna points out is that in a smaller accounting firm you are more likely to work with the person you spoke with. Larger firms can have you interview with a CPA and then you can be turned over to someone else. The problem can become that the "other" person may not be the relationship you had hoped for. Smaller firms also tend to be a little more flexible as far as hours they can meet with you, and often are less expensive to employ. While this does not always happen, it is good to be aware of it.

Big firms do have an advantage when it comes to specialized areas and other resources. If you have specific needs or want to assume more aggressive tax/accounting positions, this size firm is something to consider. They frequently will have a specialist in certain areas and other resources to tap into. You will typically pay more for a larger firm, but it may be worth it, depending on your business and concerns.

A smaller firm generally will assume a more conservative approach to bookkeeping and tax issues. This generally suits most start-up and small businesses just fine. A small firm does not mean that the product you get is less than that of a big firm. However, their overhead is typically lower, and they do tend to be more cost effective.

Some clients choose to use a smaller firm for bookkeeping and a bigger firm for taxation as they grow.

When it comes to handling bookkeeping, Shanna has discovered some of her clients have no tolerance for the paperwork side of the business. She has many clients who bring her a checkbook every month along with other receipts and information that she will use to do their monthly bookkeeping. She will tell you that whoever you choose, you need to feel comfortable with their style and keep in mind that they have access to a lot of personal information.

Taking on Your Own Books

If you decide to tackle your own bookkeeping, some of the information below will be helpful. If you decide to hire a bookkeeper, the information below will help you understand the process a bit more so you can better review your bookkeeper's work and make sure they get all the necessary receipts.

What Is Cash Flow and What Is Accrual?

One of the things your accountant needs to help you set up is the kind of record keeping you will do. The two main types are cash flow and accrual. With few exceptions, small businesses operate under a cash flow system. Here is a simple way to look at the two systems: **Cash flow** basically says if you spend it, you record it as an expense, and if you receive it, you record it as an income. The actual money spent and received represents your income and therefore is what you are taxed on. **Accrual** works differently. With accrual, you record more than money you receive or spend. You record money you are owed but haven't been paid, and likewise you record bills you owe but haven't yet paid. Your records and taxes are based on what is due rather than only what cash you have spent or income you have deposited. Both income and expenses are recorded as if the money was already in or out of your account, even though you haven't collected or paid them yet.

For small businesses, cash flow has an advantage in that you don't have to pay taxes on money you may receive, only money you have. Larger businesses often work off of an accrual basis and as your business grows, your accountant is the best person to tell you when to switch over from cash flow to accrual. However, when first starting up a business, cash flow can help keep you in the black. The black is an old accounting term derived from the concept that black ink was used to represent profits and red ink was used to record losses.

Record Keeping

In any business, you will need to keep track of all of your expense receipts and keep careful track of your income. Although for some people keeping track of these records may seem at times tedious, especially with all the other work you have when starting and running a business, the information generated from records can make or break a business.

Beyond the ShoeBox—Keeping Track of Receipts

This discussion about bookkeeping will assume you are doing a cash flow system. To make your bookkeeping easy, you need to have a checkbook and charge card or credit card that is only used for your business. These are the most common ways small business owners spend money for their business. By keeping them exclusive for your business, you can more easily record everything you spend on the business. How often you post your receipts will depend on a couple of things. One is how much business you have and the other is how much organization you have. If you have enough receipts, then post once a week. In the beginning, every two weeks may also be fine. If you are only posting once a month, then you will need to be fairly organized or not have an excessive amount of receipts.

The easiest way to do cash flow postings is to write a check (or you can charge on your card) for everything you need to buy, and to make deposits into your checking account for every cent you earn. The posting of your receipt goes in two places. The first posting will tell you if that number you just wrote down was expense or income. The second place you list that number is in a category that describes what that expense or income was all about. For example, if your puppy class that just started this week leaves you with a deposit of $1,000, then you can record that deposit as income, and also post the amount in your puppy class category. At some future time you will add up all the postings for that category so you can tell how much you've earned from your puppy classes. If that same week you wrote out a check to pay your rent, you can post that amount as an expense, then record the amount in the rent category. If those were the only transactions for the week, your bookkeeping is done for the week.

When posting purchases where you have a receipt, although the check or the charge do represent one kind of receipt, it is best to also keep that paper receipt which accompanies your purchase. You may want to write a check number or note that it was a charge, then put it into a file folder in case you need to later reference that receipt. Typically for reoccurring expenses, you make a file folder to put those receipts into. Sometimes you may classify purchases, let's say for pet supplies for resale by vendor. This way you can quickly check to see if your purchase price has gone up, meaning you need to raise your sale price to keep making the same profit. For receipts you only receive once or twice a year, a miscellaneous file may work better. However, for people who don't want to file, they can always deposit their receipts into a box, and yes, that box can even be a shoebox. It is a good idea to have a new box for each year of business. Be sure to label the box with the year and note that it is your business receipts just in case you ever need to look up a receipt. Another option is to scan in your receipts and keep those receipts in a digital file. Check the file after you scan it for readability. As with your paper receipts, you will want a different file for each year. If you have a lot of receipts, you may do file folders on your computer, much like you would with paper receipts.

Charge Cards for Expenses

As mentioned, you can use charge cards or credit cards for paying for your expenses. Charge cards and credit cards can be posted the same way you post checks that you wrote from your business checkbook. Since you need to post all your business charges, you will find this effort easier and more efficient if you have a separate card for your business. That way you may not miss a business charge that is mixed in with personal charges.

Petty Cash

There may be times when writing a check or using a charge card or credit card isn't practical. Often those kinds of purchases are small amounts of money. In those cases you need to keep, or scan, your receipt for a reimbursement. The system for reimbursements of small purchases made with cash is called petty cash. Often, these small-amount purchases are added together until they become a larger sum. At that time you can write a reimbursement check for the cash spent. When you write the check, you post each expense from your separate receipts into the correct category.

Keeping Track of Gas Mileage

Large businesses will sometimes purchase a vehicle and write off that purchase, maintenance, and insurance expenses. Small business typically can't afford to dedicate a vehicle for business usage only. Fortunately, the IRS has set up a system to accommodate using a personal vehicle for a small business. However, the IRS is a stickler about records for this. To meet their demands you will need to record your vehicle's mileage at the beginning of your business, and on the last day of the year thereafter (called ending mileage for the vehicle). You also need to keep a log of how many miles you traveled and what business reason you had for the travel. That log may be in a book you keep inside your glove box. In that book, you will record the date, the beginning mileage for the trip, the ending mileage for the trip, and the purpose of the trip. After you do the math to determine how many miles you drove, the miles are then multiplied by a rate the IRS has determined as a deduction for mileage. This rate takes into account the price of gas as well as an amount for wear and tear on the vehicle. Since gas rates can vary from year to year, the rate can also vary during the year. Your accountant can supply you with a rate to multiply your miles by and that calculation will give you a dollar-and-cent amount you can use as a mileage deduction. You can also find the rate with an online search. Just type into Google IRS mileage tax deduction. Be aware that this rate often changes year to year. For 2012, the rates were:

55.5 cents per mile for business miles driven
23 cents per mile driven for medical or moving purposes
14 cents per mile driven in service of charitable organizations

As you can see, you will be deducting different amounts for regular business than if you are donating your time by driving to a dog rescue organization. So be sure to record what your business is, as well as the date and the mileage traveled.

Computer Programs to the Rescue

At this point in time, I hope you don't feel too flooded with numbers, numbers, numbers, because for people who haven't done this process it all may seem like a lot to take in. However, once you get the process down, you will most likely find you are not spending all that much time doing your bookkeeping. Even if you do your bookkeeping the old-fashioned way, which people did years ago, and you draw lines for rows and columns and use them to keep track of your expenses and incomes (or buy tablets with those columns already drawn), this isn't an overwhelming process. But these days, there is more help for the small business owner doing their own books. That help comes in the form of computer programs that can simplify bookkeeping.

Your accountant may be a good resource as far as recommendations for a good computer bookkeeping program, or you may check with another small business owner as to what kind of program they use. Classes and online tutorials can bring you up to speed on how to use these programs. Some of their advantages are that they typically allow you, with a few clicks, to add everything up and generate a cash flow statement to easily see your profit, loss, and where you are spending most of your money. Ideally, before you decide what computer program to use, you choose

Choosing Your Software

If you are looking to buy some accounting software for your small business, here are a few considerations: The first is, does your accountant accept electronic files from this program, or will your accountant work with a printout generated from your program? Another thing to consider is your comfort level in using a program that is often determined by your ability to find an easy place to learn the program and the support team to field your questions. Finally, cost is a factor. Accounting programs can range from around forty to fifteen hundred dollars. If you'd like to get your research started with a review of accounting software for small businesses, you can find one at http://accounting-software-review.toptenreviews.com/.

ran accountant and check with them if they can readily use the program's format information to do your taxes.

Deducting Business Expenses

When you are doing your bookkeeping, you will be posting, or recording, deductible expenses. For an expense to be deductible, that expense must be both "ordinary" and "necessary." An ordinary expense is common and accepted in your field of business. For you as a dog trainer, dog equipment to help run your business will become a deductible expense. When teaching puppy classes, you may need to buy a treat bag to have on your hip when teaching. That is considered an ordinary expense. Necessary expenses are those helpful and appropriate for your business. Rent for a building where you teach the class is a necessary expense.

Personal versus Business Expenses

Most of your personal, living, and family expenses are not deductible, which probably already makes sense to you. Let's face it, although you may religiously use mouthwash and feel that you must have freshly rinsed breath every time you go to teach a class, the government isn't going to jump on the idea of you wanting to deduct the cost of your mouthwash. However, there are some areas that are less clear. For example, if you have an expense for something that is used partly for business and partly for personal purposes, then you have a deductible expense. Typically you don't deduct the entire cost from the business. Instead, you will divide the total cost between the business and personal portions. Your Internet use may be one example. If your entire family is using your Internet connection, but you are also using it for your business, then you will need to determine the percentage you use it for your business, as opposed to the usage by your family. If you only use the Internet one-third of the time for your business, then that is all you can justify as a deduction for the monthly Internet bill. You can deduct one-third of the monthly bill, but the remaining two-thirds is personal usage and is not deductible.

Home Office Deduction

You will probably have an office in some area of your home for running your home-based business. Perhaps it is an old bedroom you've converted for this kind of use. You can deduct the expense of that area, but there are specific rules to follow for that deduction. In fact, home office deduction is perhaps one of the most scrutinized areas when it comes to disallowing a deduction. So be sure to carefully follow the rules if you decide to do a home office deduction. Two rules which govern your home office deduction are: The home office must have regular and exclusive use, and this area must be the principal place for your business. In your home office, you will need to show that this area is used for helping to conduct your business, even though it will not be an area where you do your teaching. You can find a full explanation of tax deductions for your home office, by doing an online search for IRS Publication 587 (Business Use of Your Home). If you find your home office does qualify, the expenses you can deduct may include a percentage of your mortgage interest, insurance, utilities, repairs, and depreciation. The home office deduction is available for homeowners and renters, and applies to all types of homes, from apartments to mobile homes.

Understanding Balance Sheets, Income Statements, and Cash Flow Reports

When looking to understand your company's health, you can use balance sheets, income statements, and cash flow reports. Each of these tools is somewhat different and each has a different function. Even if you hire a bookkeeper or accountant to generate these information sheets, as a business owner, you need to understand what each one tells you about your business.

Your Balance Sheet

A balance sheet is also called a statement of financial position. This report is generated from the information you posted in your books (your bookkeeping) and gives you a snapshot of your financial standing. A standard balance sheet has three parts: assets, liabilities, and ownership equity. Assets are things that a company owns that have value. Assets include physical property such as your equipment, cash, and inventory.

- Assets are generally listed by how quickly they can be converted to cash. Assets that are more liquid are typically listed first. Cash is the most liquid asset. Assets such as inventory are not considered liquid because it first must be sold to claim the cash value.
- Liabilities are money that a company owes. This can include obligations such as any money borrowed to start up the business, rent for use of a building to teach your classes, any money you owed to suppliers for any

inventory you acquired, any payroll owed to employees, as well as taxes owed to the government.

■ Shareholders' equity is sometimes also called capital or net worth. The shareholders' equity represents the money that would be left if your company sold all of its assets and paid off all of its liabilities. This leftover money belongs to you as the owner of the company.

The following formula summarizes what a balance sheet shows:

ASSETS = LIABILITIES + SHAREHOLDERS' EQUITY

Basically, a company's assets have to equal, or "balance," the sum of its liabilities and shareholders' equity. You can find an example of a Balance Sheet on page 62.

Your Income Statement

The income statement is also known as a profit and loss statement. On this statement or report, you will find a total for your revenues, which is your income, and a total for your expenses listed. The expenses are subtracted from the income to tell you if you made a profit or a loss. These statements can be generated at different time intervals either weekly, or monthly, or quarterly. This tool tells you what your income was and what your expenses were for a given period of time, or another way to look at it is what did you take in and what did you keep. You will find a sample of a Monthly Income Statement on page 63.

Cash Flow Reports

After generating your profit and loss statement, and a balance sheet, it may look like the profits are coming into the business just fine. However, those two reports don't address how much cash you have readily available to use to pay the bills. That report is better tabulated in a cash flow report. The cash flow report records the amounts of cash and cash equivalents entering and leaving a company, which is also found on your profit and loss statement; however, that report also includes money coming into the business that appears on your balance sheet, such as loans. There are also cash expenditures that do not appear on your income statement, like principal payments on a loan, or inventory expenditures for items not yet sold.

Second Quarter Balance Sheet

Assets

Gross Receipts Classes		$6,450
Loan		$5,500
Agility Equipment		
Purchase price	$3,000	
Less depreciation	$150	$2,850
Office Equipment	$1,500	
Less depreciation	$75	$1,425
Total Assets		**$16,225**

Liabilities

Loan Payment	$450
Marketing	$700
Insurance	$100
Rent and Utilities	$900
Telephone and Internet	$150
Web Page Hosting	$60
Total	$2,360
Long Term Loan Debt	$9,500
Total Liabilities	**$11,860**
Owner's Equity	**$4,365**
Total Liabilities	**$16,225**

Monthly Income Statement

Assets

Gross Receipts Classes	$2,000
Total Income	**$2,000**

Liabilities

Loan Payment	$150
Marketing	$200
Rent and Utilities	$375
Telephone and Internet	$50
Web Page Hosting	$20
Office	$40
Total Expenses	**$835**
Net Profit	**$1,165**

On your cash flow report, instead of seeing large categories of income, such as the total income for all of your classes, you can see listed the individual contributions toward that total amount. For example, your profit and loss statement may show that you made $2,400 in one month from your dog training classes. But the income statement (unless you request the statement break down things more than typical) will not show the specific amounts each class contributed toward that total. That kind of a breakdown is found on your cash flow report. On that report, you will see the different amounts recorded for each class. An example of what you might find on a cash flow report would be that the puppy class was responsible for $1,000, and that the intermediate class was responsible for $800, and that your drop-in agility generated $200. This kind of detail can help you decide if you need to drop a class, do more marketing, or where to direct other efforts with your business in the future months. If you are not making the kind of net income you expected in a particular month, you can not only look at the breakdown of your income, but you can see just where you spent your money. You can then decide the best way to improve your bottom line or your profit, by deciding if you need to charge more for a class or trim your expenses in certain areas.

There may be sometimes that you find it useful to generate a weekly cash flow report. If you decide a monthly cash flow report is sufficient, a good time to generate a monthly report is after you balance your checkbook. With your report in hand, be sure to use that report to compare to your six-month cash flow projection. See if you are on target for your projection, and if not, what do you need to change? A cash flow report can help a business owner more easily discover where he or she is spending money, and the areas that are generating the most income. You can find an example of a Cash Flow Statement on page 65.

How Often to Generate These Reports

Some businesses run a balance sheet on a weekly basis and some will do it monthly to take a look at how their business is doing. For some business owners, they will find generating their balance sheet and profit and loss statement only needs to be done on a quarterly basis. This may leave you wondering how often you need to do this task. That can vary depending on a few factors. In general, when you first begin a business, unless you have a more typical than usual income (most businesses don't have a lot the first quarter) then you will probably be fine running a quarterly statement. If you find doing a balance sheet and income statement something you like, or that is easy for you to do, you may choose to do this more often. If you feel the need to evaluate your business more often, run those reports to give you a way to look at your business in a financial sense.

In the least, you will probably want to run the income statement and the balance sheet quarterly to see what kind of tax obligations you have. The income statement and the balance sheet need to be considered together when you assess your taxes. Both will feed the cash flow. There is no one magic report to get a complete picture. Everyone tends to have their favorite report that gives them a snapshot of their business. But if you are looking for a complete picture, you will need to look at all three reports.

Cash Flow May

Income

Puppy Class	$900
Agility I	$900
Drop-in Agility	$200

Total Income	**$2,000**

Expenses

Rent	$300
Utilities	$75
Telephone and I-Net	$50
Marketing	$300
Loan Payment	$150
Web Page Hosting	$20

Total Expenses	**$895**

Overall Total	**$1,105**

Inventory

Ever see year-end clearance sales? For years, businesses have held them in order to reduce inventory. That can give the illusion that inventory which is sitting idle is taxed as if it were solid income. But that isn't the situation. The IRS doesn't tax you on inventory that is just sitting there. Although you report the inventory you have, your tax liability is calculated taking into account what you started with, what you ended with, and what was your cost of goods sold. If this still seems a bit confusing, that is okay. Your accountant can help sort out the details as they impact your business. Just keep in mind that in general, having a lot of inventory that is collecting dust means you have a lot of your liquid assets tied up. It is better to keep enough inventory so you can readily make a sale, and not stock items you don't sell very often.

Cash Flow Projection

A cash flow projection is a forecast or estimate of the income you expect in the future. While the balance sheet and profit and loss statements show what actually happened in a business, the cash flow projection is only a best estimate. This may seem like a daunting task when you first begin a business, but this tool, which lists expected income and expenses, can help you manage expenditures so you don't take on too much debt in the beginning. After you do your cash flow projection, you need to post each month to see if you made that projection, if you had more than the expected income, or less than expected. Be aware that dog training is somewhat seasonal. There may be months, often around September and again just before the winter holidays, where your class attendance may decline. So include those factors in your estimates. You may want to query others who are in a similar business as to when they see declines in income. Once your business is underway, doing a cash flow projection will be more accurate and you can use it to better determine how to manage your expenses and keep your business running smoother.

Interpreting the Cash Flow Projection Sample

On page 67, you will find a six-month cash flow projection sample. This is a typical period of time to do a cash flow projection, although some people will do a one-year projection while others will project quarterly. For someone just starting out in their dog training business, six months is a good amount of time to forecast. Forecasting is the term used to estimate income and expenses used on a cash flow projection. The sample shows the thought behind how those figures were made. First off, the start-up expenses are not reflected in this projection. They were encountered a month or two before and are not part of the expenses. For that reason, you will not see posting for things like legal fees, permits, and some of the start-up office costs for this six-month cash flow projection, because those expenses occurred in November and December. This particular business owner put the effort into getting ready to open after the first of the year, because she did her research and knew that November and December are slump months when it comes to the dog training business. So she put money and work into getting ready to open her doors in January where she had a better chance of getting more students. Of course, she did market the classes over the holidays that preceded the six-month cash flow projection.

	Jan	Feb	March	April	May	June	TOTAL
Income:							
Classes	$800.00	$1,000.00	$1,500.00	$2,000.00	$2,000.00	$2,000.00	$9,300.00
Retail	$40.00	$80.00	$100.00	$120.00	$150.00	$180.00	$670.00
TOTAL INCOME	$840.00	$1,080.00	$1,600.00	$2,120.00	$2,150.00	$2,180.00	$9,970.00
Rent	$300.00	$300.00	$300.00	$300.00	$300.00	$300.00	$1,800.00
Equipment for Resale	$300.00			$300.00			$600.00
Utilities	$75.00	$75.00	$75.00	$75.00	$75.00	$75.00	$450.00
Tele and Internet	$50.00	$50.00	$50.00	$50.00	$50.00	$50.00	$300.00
Marketing	$300.00	$300.00	$300.00	$300.00	$200.00	$200.00	$1,600.00
Acct				$200.00			$200.00
Legal							
Permits/Licenses							
Repairs/Maint./Equipment						$0.00	$0.00
Seminars/Videos/Books							
Dues/Subscriptions							
Office Supplies			$50.00				$50.00
Loan Payments	$150.00	$150.00	$150.00	$150.00	$150.00	$150.00	$900.00
Web Page Hosting	$20.00	$20.00	$20.00	$20.00	$20.00	$20.00	$120.00
Insurance	$100.00			$100.00			$200.00
Income and Employment Taxes							
Sales Taxes				$13.20			$13.20
TOTAL EXPENSES	$1,295.00	$895.00	$945.00	$1,508.20	$795.00	$795.00	$6,233.20
TOTAL INCOME minus TOTAL EXPENSES	-$455	$185	$655	$611.80	$1,355	$1,385	$3,736.80

The class income is based on the concept that classes last eight weeks. The money received for the class will be paid the first day of class. What that means is that after the first class is held, you have a nice paycheck. Unfortunately, this income will not occur again for another eight weeks when that class repeats with new students, those people who have shown up seeking your help with training their dog. Since this cash flow projection begins shortly after the start of the business, the dog trainer is expecting to start two dog training classes, one a puppy class and the second an intermediate. Although only having four participants in each class isn't great, when starting out, that may be a reality. So the income for teaching the classes the first month is estimated at four people per class and starting two classes. Keep in mind that it will be two months before this class ends and another can be started, so for the puppy class and the intermediate, there will be no more income for a while.

January is a lean month. The next month, February, this dog trainer is going to begin offering two agility classes, one for beginners, and the other for intermediate dogs. Since the dog trainer has been in business a month, she hopes to have more dogs in these classes than she did in her first month's classes and has projected an income of $1,000. In March, a new puppy class begins and a new intermediate training class begins. The trainer should be able to have some of the January puppy class people enroll into the intermediate class as well as a hope to increase the puppy class number. The income for this month is expected to jump. By April, for this dog trainer, she has hit her goal of having $2,000 a month income. She feels she can teach four classes a month with ten dogs in each class. So April through June, she has reached her financial goal. Her marketing costs have reduced because her name is becoming known and she is seeing some people from her beginning classes move onto the next level of classes. She now must decide if she can increase how many classes she teaches a month by herself, or if she needs to add on another dog trainer to help.

A question you may ask yourself as you look at your cash flow compared to your cash flow projection is: "Am I charging enough for my services?" Part of that answer is rather complex in that what you charge may reflect the type of customer you are pursuing. Sometimes you will be going with an industry standard, and you may have to charge that amount. That will leave you with the task of looking over your expenses to see where you can eliminate some of the money you are spending. The cash flow report will tell you on a monthly basis what you expect to need to meet expenses. It will help flag an issue if you have overleveraged yourself.

A Healthy Perspective

You may find yourself reading some of the information in this chapter about reports several times in hopes of understanding the important business part of being a dog trainer. Even if you find yourself too busy with the other parts of getting your business up and running that you decide to turn over doing the books to an accountant or a bookkeeper, you need to save time once a month to look at your finances. At the beginning of a business, it isn't unusual to generate these reports every three months. Once you see things picking up, you may talk with your accountant about doing them more often. What I recommend, especially if this is all new to you, is that you schedule time and some money to work hand in hand with your accountant as you learn how to understand the various reports and how they impact your business plan. That is why it is critical that you find an accountant that you feel comfortable with and that can help you through your learning phase. A good accountant will help you look at where you are, where you are going, and if you are on target. Keep in mind that you will often need to have some of these reports accurately done if you decide to get a business loan, or are asking for credit from a supplier. When presenting reports to a vendor, it is appropriate to ask for a confidentiality statement to be signed to ensure your financial information isn't being shared.

Dreams Versus Reality

Ask anyone who has dealt with the reality of starting up a business and you will hear a similar story. They will all tell you that it is rare for a start-up business to make money right away. Even with good advertising, which is critical, it will take time to get clients. You need to be prepared to "carry" your business until it can support you. The average time it takes for a small business to become supporting for the sole proprietor is five years.

Expense Analysis

You may have noticed that the discussion above has only talked about income. However, on your cash flow analysis, you also list expenses. Since those expenses have not yet occurred, you are going to need to give your best estimate of what expenses you may have so you make sure your income is high enough to cover those costs. Certainly, in the beginning of a business, you have expenses even before you open the doors. To cover those costs, you either need to have saved a sufficient amount of money to cover those costs or take out some kind of loan. You will find an example for Expense Analysis on page 70. Even though these are only ideas for expenses, some of them are negotiable, meaning that if you budget one hundred dollars a month to buy books and other educational supplies, and your income isn't high enough to keep you in the black with that kind of expenditure, then you need to consider putting off that purchase until you have more income.

Taxing Issues

Yes, Benjamin Franklin had it right when he said, "In this world nothing can be said to be certain but death and taxes." For your business, you need to be aware that you will be responsible for:

- Sales tax if you sell merchandise
- Income taxes on your profits
- Self-employment taxes

Federal Identification Number

The Federal Tax Identification Number is also known as an Employer Identification Number (EIN). This number will be used for federal and state tax purposes. Most business structures need to obtain this number right away. The exception is if you are a sole proprietor who doesn't have any employees. An EIN can be obtained by filing a Form SS-4. The application for your EIN can be downloaded directly from the IRS website at www.irs.gov, or you can call the IRS at (800) 829-4933. After you fill out your application, you can fax the completed SS-4 to your state fax number that is available on the website of your secretary of state.

Sales Taxes

If you currently pay a sales tax on goods you buy at the store, then your state has a required sales tax. If you decide to have retail goods for sale to help supplement your business income, you need to apply for a sales tax license. Depending on how much revenue you generate through sales, you will need to file a report either monthly or quarterly. On that report, you will find provisions for calculating and paying other taxes you might owe including any city or county taxes.

When you buy goods for resale, you will not pay taxes on that purchase. Be sure to tell your vendor that the merchandise is for resale. They will ask for your sales tax number to record with the transaction. Some states may require you to obtain

Equipment
  Purchase
  Maintenance
  For Resale
Dues to Dog Organizations
Education
  Books or Videos
  Seminars
  Magazine Subscriptions
Rent
Utilities
Insurance
Telephone and Internet Access Fee
Office
  Computer Paper
  Printing Cartridges
  Envelopes
  Pens and Miscellaneous Office Supplies

Travel
  Mileage
  Meals
  Lodging
Bank Fees
Merchant Account Fees
Computer
  Software
  Hardware
Marketing
Web Page
  Monthly Fee
  Annual Renewal of Domain Name
  Annual Reorganization of Material
Accounting
Legal
License and Permits
Loan Payments
Income Tax

a resale certificate. To file for your sales tax number, register with your state depart-ment of revenue as a sales tax vendor. Sales tax only applies to merchandise sold. With very few exceptions, services you perform, such as dog training, are not taxed. Since sales taxes can vary from state to state, be sure to go the your state's website and investigate the information provided by the department of revenue.

Income Taxes

If you have worked for someone else as an employee, you are used to the idea that you have to pay income taxes on money you earn. Owning your own business doesn't change the fact that you have to pay taxes, it only changes the way you pay those taxes. Before, your company always made sure the government got your taxes when they were due. Now that task is up to you. Unless you have formed some kind of corporation, you will be responsible for calculating and paying in on a regular schedule your income taxes. You will pay into the federal government, and state government if you have state income taxes, on a quarterly basis. If your annual income taxes due falls under $1,000, you have the option of paying the entire amount at the end of the year. However, consider paying as you go to avoid a larger tax bill at the end of the year.

Self-Employment Taxes: Social Security and Medicare

Whether you were aware of it or not, when you worked for another company, that company paid part of your Social Security and Medicare taxes. Now that you have your own business, that will change. You will now have to pay your own Social Security and Medicare taxes without the matching funds from your place of employment. On the bright side, you will not be paying double the amount per dollar you earn compared to when you were employed by someone else. The government has a reduced amount for small business owners who are paying their own employment taxes. To pay your taxes on a quarterly basis, you will need to file a Schedule SE. If you are a sole proprietor with no employees, your Social Security Number will be used when you file your taxes. There is a wealth of tax information at the IRS website, www.irs.gov.

Paying Quarterly Taxes

When dealing with the government, quarters of the year will be: January through the end of March, April though the end of June, July through the end of September, and October through the end of December. Tax payments for those quarters are typically due on the 15th of the month following the end of the quarter. For example, the first quarter, January through the end of March, will have taxes due on April 15th.

Educational Help Outside of College Courses

With all the information about running a business, you may feel a little overwhelmed. Are you asking yourself if all successful business owners went to college before opening a business? Perhaps you wonder if there is some way to learn the business end of running a business outside of college. There is indeed. Two organizations are dedicated to helping educate the small business owners. They are SBA (Small Business Administration) found at sba.gov, and SCORE (Service Core of Retired Executives) found at score.org. Both organizations offer a lot of information and help for the small business owner and classes on pertinent topics for little or no fee.

Insurance has become a necessary part of our everyday lives. Homeowners have homeowner insurance, auto insurance is required for drivers, and many renters carry rental insurance. Becoming a business owner means you will need to expand your insurance coverage. Below are different kinds of insurance and what role they need to play in your business. Be sure to contact your local insurance agent about your specific needs based on the size and scope of your business.

Homeowner Insurance Extensions or Independent Policies

The other day I was talking to another dog business owner and we got into the topic of insurance. She told me that she put a rider onto her home owner's insurance that covered her equipment and the liability for her dog business. I had a similar policy years ago for my business, but after I expanded my business I acquired separate business insurance for my home-based dog training business. After my dog friend told me she was getting a better deal, I called my insurance agent, looking to see if I too could save some money by expanding my homeowner's policy (called adding a business rider) instead of having a separate insurance policy. That phone call gave me a very important education on insurance as well as a warning about pitfalls.

It appears that several things have changed in recent years regarding insurance. You will find that some homeowner's insurance companies may not want to have you as a client any longer should you decide to operate a home-based dog training business out of your house. Even if you have separate insurance, some homeowner insurance companies don't want to take the liability risk. Most homeowner insurance companies don't mind if you have an office in a bedroom where you engage in paperwork, but they do show concerns if you have clients coming and going from your residence.

For that reason don't look to your homeowner's policy as a way of covering your business insurance needs, even if you want to add a business rider to your policy. I spoke with a couple of insurance agents about my friend's situation, and both said they had concerns about this woman's policy, stating these days homeowner insurance companies don't want to cover your dog training business, even with a business rider. I recommend you seek independent business insurance for your insurance needs. Although some insurance companies have different departments for both homeowner's insurance and for home-based business insurance, I found the best solution was to use an independent insurance agent who understands the insurance needs of a dog training business.

Adequate coverage is key. You need to sit down and talk over what you plan on doing in your business. If, in the future, you change the services you offer or how you conduct your business, be sure to contact your insurance agent for a business insurance review. My business insurance includes coverage when I transport a dog, or if I were to board a dog for training at my house, and completed operations coverage that will cover me if one of the dogs I train at some time in the future bites someone and the dog owner decides I am at fault. Although most dog trainers know that isn't the case, you still need coverage. My coverage is for up to two million dollars and falls under my general liability, which is two million per occurrence, and includes a four million dollar aggregate. Before my liability insurance is engaged on an incident, I have ten thousand dollar no-fault medical coverage for any one person that covers small incidents that don't need to involve my general liability. My policy includes coverage for any building I rent for up to three hundred thousand dollars if for any reason the building sustained damage associated with me. And if another trainer decided to sue me for libel, slander, or defamation of character, I'm covered.

In general, homeowner's policies with business riders are not really designed to be adequate enough coverage for people in the dog business. Although operating as an LLC does give you some liability protection, if you train dogs on your property, don't expect the liability coverage on your homeowner's policy to cover anything and be aware that most have a business exclusion. If you get sued, you will need liability through some kind of business insurance. Be sure the agent you use specializes in covering small businesses and has experience in the needs of a dog training business.

Automobile Insurance

States regulate the fact that you need automobile insurance for your car. It is important you understand how that insurance does and doesn't impact your business. If you are in an accident, either with or without dogs in your vehicle, your insurance will cover your car, and any liability for damage for other vehicles, even if you are found at fault. Depending on your state and your specific policy, you may or may not have medical coverage for any injuries you sustain in that accident. As for any dogs that are injured, covering animals is not the goal of this kind of policy. Even if you have a dog trailer in tow and have paid for trailer insurance, typical automobile policies are concerned with returning the vehicle and the vehicle in tow back to its original state. Contents inside are not covered by vehicle policies.

If your dog training business involves transporting dogs of any kind for clients, you will need specialized insurance such as kennel pro coverage to protect dogs and the dog's value. Be sure your specialty insurance covers the value of the dogs transported. For example, if you tend to transport several Labrador Retrievers, and those dogs are valued at twenty thousand dollars each because of their breeding and training, be sure your insurance agent has a clear picture of the value of the dogs you transport.

Liability Insurance

Your business needs liability insurance as a protection against lawsuits. There are several kinds of liability insurance available for businesses, including insurance for providers of professional services, and product liability insurance for product manufacturers. In a dog training business, your liability insurance first and foremost needs to cover you for professional services. However, there are other liabilities you must consider. You must consider liability should an animal become injured. You also need insurance should a person become injured. Perhaps you have two people in a training class and one person's dog bites another person. You will find that you can become a target for liability. Even if all you teach are puppy classes, unexpected incidences can happen, no matter what kind of precautions you take. There is also the matter that in today's society, there is the tendency to blame others for mishaps we sometimes cause ourselves. Dog owners who are acting negligently when at a class may turn blame on you, even when they are clearly at fault. This can also happen when you do home visits for a dog behavior issue. Unfortunately, legal judgments don't always follow along the lines of common sense, but more often tend to be the

A good insurance broker is experienced in hunting around different agencies to find the best insurance deal. Dennis Stowers, of Mourer-Foster Agency, has more than the usual finesse when it comes to locating the right insurance plan, because he is more than the usual dog owner. Dennis has had hunting dogs since he was sixteen, and has trained, campaigned, and competed with his dogs.

Dennis brings his unique dog savvy to his work and over the years he has honed his expertise in insuring dog-related businesses. He began insuring dog businesses about fifteen years ago, when he was approached by a woman with a pet sitting business. At that time, this was unique. Dog sitting businesses were a new phenomenon and regular insurance brokers didn't have solid ideas as to all the angles needed to adequately insure a dog-based business. As a broker, Dennis did research and found a company for that pet sitter's general liability. Soon, he found that others in the dog business were calling him to help with their insurance needs. Even the APDT contacted him to invite him to their annual convention where he set up a booth in their commercial hall.

Over the years, Dennis has let his customers' unique needs become his teacher. He states that a lot of insurance companies don't do a very good job at offering exactly what the dog trainers need. For example, a dog trainer needs more than coverage for a building. Dog trainers may modify a building, making the replacement cost greater than an average building. For example, the setup for a training area or kenneling area can vary in value, and will need different coverage than a structure that merely houses supplies. There are other considerations for a dog trainer to get complete coverage of a specific business. A common question he asks his clients is whether they transport dogs, and if they house dogs they are training. A regular liability policy may not cover these issues. Dennis will tell you right out that for a business to be adequately covered, the agent and/or broker needs to ask the right questions to help draw out the real exposures of a dog training business. Because this kind of communication is so vital, Dennis will not take an application over the Internet. He feels if he doesn't talk to people and feel out their real needs, then he can't make sure he gives them adequate coverage.

Dennis's job doesn't end after he writes a policy. Behind the scenes, he is always looking at how his client's needs are changing. These insights often arise from other client's insurance claims that he has worked to resolve. He uses those issues to tailor specific coverage needed in different dog businesses into the base policy. This helps to create coverage which is more complete, but still obtainable at a reasonable cost.

Dennis recommends that any dog training business owner find an agent they can deal with one on one, and expect that agent to ask them questions they hadn't considered. That way they can get the real coverage they need. Find someone with experience in your field. There is one thing Dennis will caution you about if you decide to contact him: If it is October, he may sneak out a day here or there to go hunting with his dogs. But any other time he is willing to answer questions about insurance.

result of which lawyer is more clever. Be sure to consult with your agent/broker and explore what kind of liability exposure you have in your business so that your policy coverage is adequate. A typical amount of liability coverage for a dog trainer is two million dollars.

Business Interruption Insurance

Business interruption insurance isn't included in a regular dog trainer insurance policy, but is a separate insurance you may or may not decide to pursue. To help determine if you need this coverage, you need to look closely at your operation. If you are renting space, think about how your business may be impacted if something happened to that building. Could you find, in a reasonable period of time, a new place to set up your business? If this is true, then save your money on business interruption insurance. However, if you get into a dog training facility where you have gone to the expense of putting down mats and if you have a lot of equipment you store at that facility because moving it around isn't practical, you may want to investigate business interruption insurance. If interruption of your business is going to mean your only means of income is now gone, this kind of insurance would warrant further investigation.

Business interruption insurance typically covers clients for up to one year. However, keep in mind that if you had to cease your business for about a year, you will probably need some additional time to build your clientele back up. Make sure your insurance can make provision for that kind of situation.

Workman's Compensation

A workman's compensation policy provides wage replacement and medical benefits for employees who are injured in the course of employment, in exchange for relinquishment of the employee's right to sue his or her employer for negligence. If you are a sole proprietor, you often have a choice on taking out this kind of insurance. Many states will let you opt out of workman's comp. If you already have an adequate health insurance policy, then opting out can keep you from paying for the same coverage twice, especially since workman's compensation will not cover any injuries or health issues not directly caused by your work. So if you are your only employee, you may be better served by putting your money in a good heath insurance policy that covers you both during and outside of work.

When it comes to your employees, if they are regular employees, you need to cover them under a workman's comp policy. In addition to workman's compensation, with regular employees, you will be also paying Social Security and withholding taxes. However, some dog training business owners hire independent contractors or subcontractors to teach classes. Business owners can get into issues with the independent or subcontractors. There are specific rules for independent contractors, discussed in more detail in chapter 13. If your employee is an independent or subcontractor, you have one of two choices: You can require him to carry his own workman's compensation and have him give you an up-to-date proof-of-insurance certificate, or you can include him in your policy and charge him for the insurance. When you hire independent or subcontractors, the obligation to carry workman's compensation is supposed to fall on their shoulders. However, should they fail to carry this insurance and if they should get hurt on the job, you may find yourself in a financial obligation you didn't bargain for. They can come back against you and if they do, you can find yourself with no insurance to cover their claim. Even if you win your case in court that they are a true independent or subcontractor and you are not responsible, your lawyer fees will not be reimbursed. Many times courts tend to rule against the business owners in many of these cases.

Do You Need an Independent Insurance Agent?

If you own a car or a home, and sometimes even if you rent, you already have insurance. Often these policies are written by many of the agencies you see advertised on television such as Farmers or American Family Insurance. Typically, you deal with an agent who writes insurance for only one company and you call him your American Family Insurance, or Farmers, agent. However, there are some agents who write for several different insurance companies. These agents are called independent agents. When you work with an independent agent, there can be an advantage in that the agent can price around as well as search around for the best coverage for your needs. Yet another kind of agent is called an insurance broker. Although some people use the terms independent insurance agent and insurance broker interchangeably, they actually have two different purposes. Since insurance companies have a cost involved with the agents who write policies for them, some agents and insurance companies never form a relationship. If your independent agent doesn't write enough policies for a particular company, but he feels he needs to use a company he doesn't have a relationship with, he may turn to an insurance broker to secure your policy. That broker will have access to a company the independent agent does not. No matter who you choose to use for your insurance needs, make sure your agent has a good understanding of your business and your insurance needs. You may want to seek a recommendation from other dog business owners.

Back to the Business Plan

Remember that business plan you wrote? It discussed different directions you may take your business in the future. If you initially didn't plan on boarding dogs for training but have now modified your business plan, you need to also modify your business insurance.

07

Banking on Your Future

As a business owner, you will need to set up accounts to handle your business checking, and you will probably want to have a business charge card or a business credit card. When dealing with money you receive through your business, you may want to arrange to accept charge cards or credit cards. At this time, credit unions are not allowed to handle business checking accounts, though that may change in the future. Until then, your business banking will be done through a retail or commercial bank.

Checking and Savings Accounts

As a business owner, you will need a separate checking account. Currently banks are the institutions you must deal with for checking accounts. As mentioned already, at this time, credit unions are not permitted to have checking accounts for business. I personally hope that changes soon. I am much happier with my current credit union than I have been with any bank. The reason is cost. Credit unions offer checking for free. Banks want to charge for checking accounts. How much a bank charges can vary from bank to bank. Some will charge a monthly fee, and also may charge a fee for every check that clears your account. You will find you can save money on your checking account by doing a little shopping around. Check with several banks in your area. Sometimes smaller, more local banks may offer you the best deal.

Once you do find your ideal bank, you will be ordering checks. There are a lot of different designs you can have on your checks from humorous to more businesslike in appearance. You can even have pictures printed on them. It is a poor idea to have checks printed with anything that suggests humor when you want people to take your business seriously. Likewise, floral or decorative designs will not paint the right picture for your business. A picture of a dog is fine, but since this won't often help in marketing your business, having an extra picture printed on a check, if it costs too much, may not be a wise expenditure. Look into the standard business check designs and pick one that looks professional. Since banks tend to charge more if you order checks through them, don't hesitate to check online to see if you can find a better deal on your checks. Perhaps you will save enough so that you can afford that picture of a dog or your logo.

When it comes to depositing checks written to you, buy a self-inking stamp that has your business name, your account number if the bank requires that, and the words "for deposit only." This will make your banking easy and if you get in the habit of stamping all checks immediately, your checks will be safer if you keep them in a drawer a day or two before depositing them.

In your personal life, you may be used to having both a checking and a savings account. This may or may not serve you as a business. Some people keep all their money in a checking account until it is time to disperse the money for payments. This is a practice that will serve you well. However, if you have expenses that occur once or twice a year, and you want to determine at a glance how much cash in your checking account is readily available, you may decide to use a savings account. You can make deposits in your savings account for those annual or other periodic charges, such as your business insurance or anticipated tax payments. This will better allow you at a glance at your checking account balance to determine if you have a little extra money for that extra equipment purchase you may want. By allocating on a regular basis the money you need for periodic expenses, you will not come up to your payment time short on funds.

Checks as Receipts

One of the great things about checks is that by writing them, you have a receipt. It is a good idea to get the kind of checks that produce an automatic copy when you write your check. That way if you tear out a check you may have written while distracted by a student or something else, and you to forget to put a note in your check register, you have a record of who you wrote the check to and the amount. When writing a check, you will find it a good idea to use the memo line. Jot a short note that will help you categorize the expense later on. Remember, checks become a way of keeping track of your business expenses, so be sure to use your checking account exclusively for business.

Charge Cards and Credit Cards

Do you have a charge card or a credit card? Do you know the difference between a charge card and a credit card? A charge card requires you to pay your balance in full when the statement is due and a credit card will allow you to carry a balance, but will charge you interest on that balance. It seems that almost everyone has one of those kinds of cards. Some people have both charge and debit cards. There are two perspectives with dealing with charge cards or credit cards and debit cards for a business. The first is your usage for acquiring merchandise, or making payments with your card. The second is taking charge or credit cards or debit cards from your customers. The first part of the discussion below will focus on you as a small business owner using charge cards or credit cards or debit cards for purchases and using credit cards as loan tools and for cash flow. The second part of the discussion will entail how to set up to accept charge or credit and debit cards from your customers.

Charge Cards and Debit Cards Help Manage Your Cash Flow

Many businesses these days find using charge cards to acquire goods very handy. Charge cards or credit cards are sometimes more welcomed at businesses than checks because checks can have issues with insufficient funds. By using a charge card or credit card for business purchases, you can use your receipt to post to your books, just like you post a check. You can also use a debit card like a check. Right now, swiping a debit card rather than writing a check doesn't cost extra fees, but some banks are wanting to change that. If you do decide to use a debit card, make sure you have a good way of keeping track of your receipts so you can post to your books.

Carrying a Balance on Your Business Charge Cards

Debit cards are designed to take money directly out of your checking account, whereas a credit card allows you to have access to money that isn't in an account. An ideal situation is that every month you pay off your credit card balance. This prevents you from incurring interest on your purchases and keeps down your overall costs. If you find that at the end of the month, due to an unexpected expense you need to carry a balance on your card, keep in mind that carrying a balance means you just took out a short-term loan. That being said, some businesses find carrying a loan on their credit card as one way to help with start-up cash. The disadvantage is that credit cards tend to carry a higher interest rate. For that reason, if you need help short term on cash flow, go ahead and use your card. A good rule of thumb is if you have a credit card, you need to have a pay-off plan. If your short-term need turns into a longer-term need, you may be better served by looking into other options for financing. Chapter 8 talks more about some of the options for financing a business.

The American Express Small Business Credit Card

Sometimes your cash flow issues only span a short period of time. For those kinds of cash flow issues, some small business owners grab their credit card and carry a balance for a while. Unfortunately, any interest paid during that time only takes away from the bottom line. American Express has offered another solution for this kind of short-term expense. They call their card a Plum Card. At this time, the card is offered for the first year for free, followed by an annual fee of $185. Many business owners feel this card has advantages they need, even though they have to pay that annual fee. What this card offers is to allow you to have up to sixty days after the statement closing date to pay off a balance without paying any interest. They do require a 10 percent payment of the balance to secure this grace period. There is no spending limit. If you happen to pay off your balance within ten days of your statement's closing date, you can earn a 1.5 percent early payment discount that can help offset the annual fee. Some vendors will extend a discount to people using this card. Plum Card includes extra cash back rewards from participating open Network merchants. To find out what merchants are in the network, and how much discount you can receive, you first go to www.opensavings.com. There you will find an orange tab that says Explore All Partners. When you click on that tab, you will arrive at a web page that lists the participating merchants. When you click on a merchant, you find out how much of a discount they offer. You might consider the Plum Card as an option, both for the merchant discounts and because many training classes are on about a sixty-day cycle. Using the grace period until you collect for your next class may save you interest in the long run.

Accepting Charge or Credit Cards or Debit Cards as Payments

Taking charge cards, credit cards, or debit cards can actually increase your sales. Many people find using plastic much easier than writing a check. And these days, fewer and fewer checks are written. If you have a client all fired up about buying some equipment, but they don't have their checkbook, chances are you will lose that sale.

Some of your clients are more likely to buy classes if you make it easier by accepting a charge card or credit card.

Unfortunately, accepting a client's charge, credit, or debit card is not free for you. There are several fees you need to pay for each swipe and you will need a way to capture the charge card or credit card number. Here are a few ways merchants can accept charge card or credit cards. One way is to have a phone line at your training facility. You can buy or rent a small card swiping device and use that to enter charge card or credit card data. After that, the line dials up and you enter an amount. Once you get that card accepted, the transaction is completed. If you don't have a phone line available, another option is to use a wireless card swiping device. But keep in mind this method requires a monthly fee for wireless access on top of the charge for either buying or renting the card swiper. Yet another way is to arrange to enter the card number on your computer. Assuming you have Internet access, this method doesn't require a separate purchase or rental of a card swiping machine. All of these methods cost different amounts, something you can investigate by calling several merchant card providers.

No matter how you arrange to capture the card number, there are other fees involved with a charge card or credit card merchant account. Typically, you will have to pay a monthly fee to the company who has your merchant account. This fee is charged no matter what kind of sales you have. Each sale you make has a transaction fee along with a percentage charged of the sale. For example, if you sold a dog collar for ten dollars, you can expect to pay a transaction fee when you swipe that card along with a fee based on a percentage of the total amount. Both of those charges are in addition to your monthly fee, and don't include the purchase or rental of a card swiping device. However, you still may find that accepting charge cards or credit cards can increase your sales enough to justify these costs.

You need to shop around to find out who has the best deal for you and your type of business. When you price out your merchant account, ask if there is a difference in the fees for different kinds of cards. It isn't unusual for regular charge cards or credit cards to have the least expensive transaction fee; however, if the card has reward points earned by the cardholder, you may have a higher transaction fee. If your demographic is an area where most of your customers have these kinds of cards, you may want to shop around for a company that charges a flat rate for all cards, even if that transaction fee is higher for the non-reward cards. Also be aware that if your customer is using their business card to pay for your class or buy merchandise, you will pay more fees for that kind of card. Make sure you get a good explanation of all the fees to better decide which merchant account company is going to work the best for you. Keep in mind that it is not automatic that you need to be able to accept charge cards or credit cards. If you are not selling any merchandise, you may not find this an advantage. One good criterion is to ask yourself if taking charge cards or credit cards will increase business. If your customers are not walking away because you don't offer this convenience, then accepting cash or checks can help keep down your overhead costs. For those of you wondering if credit cards are the only financing available, chapter 8 has some other options to consider.

08

Financing Your Training Business

Have you been saving money from your day job to start up your dog training business? Or do you plan on getting some kind of financing? Even if you hope to "pay as you go" for the business, you need to get a good idea of how much things will cost. Some of the information in the preceding chapters has already helped prep you to gather ideas that will help you work through figures for your expenses. Although costs will vary according to your specific business, below are some considerations when figuring out what your business will cost.

What It Will Cost

When it comes to estimating costs for your business, there are a lot of variables. But if you take a systematic approach, you can better and more accurately secure a good estimate. You will need to take the time and effort to thoroughly think though what things will cost to keep your business finances on track.

Let's see how expenses can be figured out by looking at an example. A good way to begin is to start at the biggest expenses first. For most dog trainers their biggest expenses are typically acquiring equipment and acquiring a place to do their training. Let's take the example of deciding to convert your garage into a puppy training classroom. Since this is an already constructed area, you may hope this will be a relatively inexpensive venture, simply park the cars outside of the garage and you are almost done. But you will need to consider a few more factors. Heating and cooling are one consideration. You can probably get away with opening doors and putting up a portable fence as a barrier in the summer and not have to worry about keeping the garage cool. However, in the winter, you need to come up with a plan to heat the place.

Using a space heater may not be practical unless you can locate them out of "doggy" harm's way. Although there are heaters that can be mounted in the corner of the garage, the initial investment will be a bit more money than a few space heaters. When looking into things, such as heating a garage, you need to look at initial costs from a few perspectives. When deciding if purchasing a few space heaters is a better way to do your heating, take into account both the initial purchase price as well as how much these devices take to run. If you plan on teaching from your garage for one year, a quick initial purchase of space heaters along with the cost of the electricity might tell you that this is less expensive than having a gas-mounted unit developed for heating garages in the corner of the garage.

But don't stop short at supplying heat. Typically, garages aren't insulated. If you are looking to heat the garage for a few hours not having insulation may be okay, or you may need a few extra heaters to try and keep things warm. Perhaps you will decide to insulate the garage. That will of course be a cost you need to bid out before you make a final decision if that cost warrants your energy savings. One added expense you may run into is that many building codes require a special foil lined insulation to be installed in a garage area and that costs more than regular insulation. The other question is: Should you cover the insulation? Sheet rock costs money, and so does taping and painting it. Oh, and did I mention you may need to get a building permit? And gosh, you haven't even bought dog mats for the floor yet. Does this all of a sudden seem a bit more complicated? Take heart. At this stage in the game, by sitting down and working through what things will actually cost, you may save yourself difficulty later. With a project such as converting a garage into a heated area, you will find that by working through the logistics of what you need to do, you can not only get a better feel for how much something is likely to cost, but that this kind of project will take some time to complete. This may lead you to decide to only teach classes in the summer from your garage to eliminate any heating issues, and arrange to rent space from a doggy day care center during the winter months. Oh, and don't forget that if you are teaching after dark, you will probably need to add more lighting. By carefully working through what things will cost, you can better launch yourself into a successful start for your business.

Bidding Work Out

Should you find that you need to collect costs for a project, you will need to do what is known as bid things out, or get a bid for work. When I looked into converting a garage for doggy use where I needed insulation and heating, I was unpleasantly surprised to get one bid for insulation from a company that didn't know it needed to use foil insulation. Of course their bid was far less. You will find that it is a good idea to get at least three bids on any work you need done, and to carefully look over those bids.

Hint: When I work through things such as how much something will cost for a business, I often find that brainstorming with someone else helps keep me from missing things. I am fortunate to have a husband with a keen mind for such things. I also sometimes consult with my brothers who have worked in construction. When working through figures, don't hesitate to put on a pot of coffee, set out a few cookies, and invite in some help.

Storage Unit Conversion

In chapter 10, I talk about one of the first places I did dog training. The facility was located in a commercial storage shed. Even though many of these may or may not be insulated, they seem a bit easier to heat. Some may come with heating already in place. But these units will not always be ready for you to simply walk into and set up shop. You may need to supply some kind of bathroom facility as well as put down dog mats. Those dog mats will need to be replaced from time to time, so when doing your cost estimates, keep that in mind. Often, if you are looking into converting a storage area into a business area, it's best to locate in a storage unit that already has other business conversions. You would be best served to visit several other dog training facilities and jot notes. If you can find someone who has a knack for this kind of thing, be sure to bring them along to help you gather information. Don't hesitate to buy them lunch for their time. At lunch, you can review details of your information gathering expedition. Oh, and don't forget that since that meal discusses business, it is a tax deduction. So keep your receipt and mark on the back what business was discussed with whom.

Does it seem like you are being nudged toward renting space that you don't need to convert? For many that will be a good solution when they are first beginning their business. But not all. One dog trainer had saved for her business to accommodate converting a storage area into a dog training facility. She also made sure she had enough revenues to carry herself for a couple of years until the business could make it on its own. This worked well for her. If you don't have a sum of money or the means to put away like that individual did, but are determined to construct your own training facility, then perhaps a loan is a consideration.

Small Business Loans

Perhaps your goals for starting your new business are falling short when it comes to adequate financing. Or perhaps you began your business small, but now have found an opportunity for growth. Unfortunately, you lack the funds to get that expanded growth underway. Small business loans are what many people turn to when looking for financing. Banks are often the first place we think about when looking for a loan. The US Small Business Administration is certainly an option to investigate. Private investors are another place to look when seeking financing outside of your own means. There are several considerations before you decide if loans are right for your business, which kind is best for you, and where to get your financing.

One question which may have occurred to you is if it is better to get a loan when you are first starting up this kind of business, or to wait until you are well underway and looking to expand. If you anticipate needing money to keep your business going in your first year or two, you need to secure this money before you open your doors. There is a reluctance to loan money to a business that isn't making ends meet, as opposed to one that is looking to expand or one which is looking to start. As to how much money, or even if you need money for the first couple of years, that information can be better determined by looking at your business plan and doing your cash flow projection. Be aware that most banks will expect that a home-based business like this, since it is a service business, will not need a lot of start-up cash. After all, if you are teaching classes, you will be paid for the class before you do the service and your home office will not cost nearly as much as rented office space. Even if you want to work out of a facility for teaching your classes, there are a lot of options other than trying to buy or convert your own building. If you do feel you need to secure a loan, below is some information on different kinds of loans.

Bank Loans

You will find that banks will do two major kinds of loans you can use for your business: One is a secured loan, and the other is an unsecured loan. Secured loans are those that have some kind of asset the bank can confiscate should you default on your loan. Unsecured loans don't have any assets to secure the loan, making them harder for you to secure. But that doesn't mean they can't be arranged.

Secured Loans

A secured bank loan is one that you as a borrower have secured with some kind of asset such as real estate, or stocks and bonds. Common examples of secured loans are home loans or a car loan. Banks prefer to loan money for secured loans over unsecured loans making secured loans easier for you to obtain.

One kind of secured loan you may want to check into is a home equity line of credit. If you have equity in your home, this kind of loan can allow you access to money for your business as you need it. Another kind of money you can get from your home is a second mortgage. With a second mortgage, you take out a sum that reflects your home equity when you close on the loan. Once you have the money, you can't obtain any more from that loan. The loan is paid off in installments much like a first mortgage. Both kinds of loans use your home as security. Having enough start-up money can help you buy equipment and pay bills through those first few years when you struggle to earn enough in your new business to make ends meet. This kind of available capital can also help you if you have a few slow months. The interest rate for a second mortgage is set at the time you obtain the loan. With the home equity line of credit, the interest rate is tied into the prime rate. Even at its worst over the last ten years, the prime has been far below what you can get with a credit card. Even though a home equity line of credit is less expensive money to use for your business, be cautious as to how much of your equity you tap into. Make sure you will have the income to cover a regular payment and that your financial statements agree with your expenditure. In the end you will need to pay this back in full or risk losing your home.

Another kind of secured bank loan is one where you use stocks or bonds to secure the loan. Be aware that a loan secured with stocks or bonds carries a caution. If you max out the value of your stocks or bonds used to secure the loan, and the stock market takes a dive, then the bank will want you to immediately come up with some cash to cover the unsecured part of the loan.

Unsecured Loans

Some people have the attitude that, with the exception of a secured loan, banks don't want to loan money for small businesses. That isn't true. What is true is that banks will not want to loan you money to pay your own salary in a business. They also will show a lot of caution when loaning money. After all, with no security they need to feel certain that you have the ability to pay back your loan.

A bank will not want to loan you money without a good business plan. They look at your business plan to assess if you have the ability to run this business and to pay them back. A business loan from a bank is a more complex process than taking out an auto or home loan. With auto and home loans, the lender merely needs to check some common items and stamp an approval. A small business loan falls under a lot more scrutiny. In addition to your business plan, the bank will want your personal financial statement, a resume where you show what kinds of experience you bring for running this kind of business, income tax returns, and business licenses. Since this process is so much more involved than other kinds of loans, banks typically want to deal with larger amounts of money when doing a business loan. They simply can't charge enough to give you a small loan. So if you are looking for a loan under fifty thousand dollars, this is probably not the kind of loan for you.

Banks typically are more interested in loaning money to people they already know, so go first to a bank you already have a relationship with. If that bank turns you down, don't immediately give up. Try other banks in the area. Banks weigh in a lot of factors when deciding if they will loan a small business money. One of those factors is their current amount of loans and how healthy those current loans are. So don't stop at the first "no" you get.

Small Business Loans from the Government

Perhaps you've heard about small business loans available through the government. One place to start your loan investigation is to look into loans and grants under sba.gov. Federal, state, and local governments offer a wide range of financing programs to help small businesses start and grow their operations. These programs include low-interest loans, venture capital, and scientific and economic development grants. There is a loan and grants search tool online, but none of the categories include service industries, in which a dog training business is classified.

One of the government-backed small business loan programs is called the 7(a) Loan Program. This is a loan that the bank applies for on your behalf. There is a charge for that application which you will pay the bank. If you are approved, the bank handling the loan will have the safety factor so that if you do default on this loan, they are covered for up to 80 percent, much like borrower's insurance for home loans.

Is Credit Card Financing Practical?

Some people use a credit card to help finance the upstart for a small business. At first glance that may not seem like a very good idea. After all, credit cards are not known for providing the best interest rates. But for some businesses, this can work as a way to generate start-up cash, or even to help ride over a seasonal slowdown in the business. As to how much of a loan balance is feasible to carry on a credit card before you look toward more permanent financing, that is, in part, a personal thing. For some people up to ten thousand dollars is their comfort zone. In general, one shouldn't go over twenty thousand dollars with this kind of financing. More information about specialty business credit cards that better accommodate short-term loans is in chapter 7.

Are Investors a Solution?

Yet another option for financing a business is to find investors to help fund your business. In general, investors traditionally are more willing to take a risk than banks. The first place to look for an investor is to investigate business associates or even acquaintances you know. If you don't personally know anyone who has money to invest in a start-up business, then look in your community. People are often more willing to invest in something locally then outside their area. Expect to approach an investor the same way you would a bank. Gather your financial information and put together a well-groomed business plan. Don't be surprised if your potential investors want a bit of a sales pitch for your business.

Avoid a Loan Error

One mistake you need to avoid is to try to begin a business on a shoestring budget. So after figuring up how much you will need to launch and carry your business through the two or three years, if you come up short, you might want to look into a loan. If you launch your business and discover that you need additional income for survival that first year, or even two, you will find lenders have a lot of reluctance to loan money to a business that isn't able to pay the bills. So take the time to calculate your expenses and carefully create that business plan. If you see the possible need for money to succeed, apply before you have the actual need.

These days, the Internet seems to be the place to locate everything. It is also a place you may want to look for investors. But be cautious. The Internet can also host sites that are actually clever scams that will take your money, instead of help you obtain money. You should never expect to pay a fee up front when looking for an investor, other than a small fee for posting your information. If you do decide to check out investors online, do a lot of investigating before you proceed with this opportunity. Look for recommendations from other people. Be sure to personally e-mail a few of them to be sure they are legitimate.

Where to Buy Supplies

Finding supplies for your business will be driven, in part, by both quality and cost. With the Internet so easy to use to locate deals, you will probably find yourself doing a bit of web searching. Keep in mind that prices between suppliers can vary a lot. Although it won't pay to put in a lot of time searching for the best deal on every item, on your big purchases you will need to locate the best deal. A year ago when I went to bid out purchasing some additional agility jumps, like many people, I used the Internet to search. I was quite surprised to find the variability in prices. But I didn't simply grab at the first lowest price. There are too many other factors I needed to consider than just the initial price. Some clever suppliers have learned how to lower their initial price, but make up for that money in the shipping. Before making that final purchase decision, I made sure I added up the total shipped cost before deciding which was the best deal.

Quality is more important to you as a business owner than it is as an average dog owner. Your equipment needs to be durable enough to take a lot of wear and tear. Before making a major purchase, you might try and network with some other dog trainers. Going out of state to contact those trainers may help you find people more willing to talk to you, since you don't pose an immediate competition threat. When buying items such as dog mats, you need good durability, or the time and money you spend replacing poorer quality mats can set you back with your business endeavors. Another place to check out equipment is to search for complaints online.

When purchasing equipment, don't rule out local opportunities. Oftentimes you can find out about these at dog events. Even if you don't want to go to a local show to watch, go to the booths to see if someone is offering equipment that is manufactured locally. Get their flyers and check their prices. Don't forget you'll save on shipping if you can go and pick the equipment up. And don't forget to work to negotiate a discount.

Guidelines about Selling Merchandise

We've already discussed some about carrying supplies to sell to customers. It makes a lot of sense that if you find too many people showing up to your class with the wrong kinds of equipment, that you can benefit by carrying more ideal equipment such as dog collars and leashes to sell. Even treat bags can be a frequently bought item. These kinds of items need to be readily available to monopolize the sales opportunity. Since your initial investment isn't all that large, should you not sell equipment for a month or two, that won't bother your bottom line a lot, as long as you don't stock large quantities of the smaller equipment. So be sure to increase your stock slowly until you get a feel for the salability of different items.

When it comes to larger items, trying to stock things such as an agility tunnel can tie up a lot of cash. What you can do instead is arrange to sell without inventory. The first thing you need to do to achieve this sales opportunity is to find a supplier who will sell you your initial equipment at wholesale or a discounted price. Then, you can post equipment information at your training facility so your students know they can buy the very same equipment they are using to train with in your class. If someone decides to buy, let's say a dog walk, you can make the order when you accept the student's payment for the equipment. Check with your supplier to see if you have to have the merchandise delivered to your training area, or if you can have the supplier ship directly to people's homes. You might also want to set up an opportunity for people to "group" order at the end of each class. By bundling the orders, your students can buy equipment through you, which can generate your business extra money, and also saves your students on their shipping because of the bundling of the order. This becomes a win/win for both of you. Keep in mind bundled orders will need to be delivered to one location such as your training facility.

Setting Your Prices

Before you set your prices, you need to gather some information. First off, you need to find out what the prices are of your competitors. Then you need to find out how your services compare. Finally, you need to think about what kind of clientele you plan on marketing to.

With a few phone calls and some visits to a few websites for other trainers in your area, you can begin to get an idea of what other dog trainers are charging for classes or for private consultations. One good place to begin your research is at the chain pet supply stores that offer classes. These places often offer less expensive opportunities. Find out the cost for a class, how many weeks the class lasts, and find out something about what you can expect the dog to learn. This will give you a comparable for when you price out your classes. Next, call and/or visit websites for other dog trainers in the area. Once you gather your pricing and class content information, ask yourself who you want to market to—simply saying "dog owners" isn't enough. You need to look at the demographics of the area. Ask yourself what are the population needs, what are they willing to pay, and can you motivate them to take your classes? Sometimes a dog trainer can charge a higher price because that trainer can market to a clientele willing to pay a higher price. Not everyone is looking for a bargain, and some will not want the lowest-priced deal. In general, you will find that classes are a set fee such as eight classes for $120 (prices will vary in different locations and intervals and total weeks will with the class). Private consultations are often a half-hour or one-hour rate, but can also be sold as a package deal where you do a given number of consultations for a set fee.

As a neophyte, to attract clients, a discount can be helpful. Don't be too eager to price yourself below everyone else, and then plan on raising prices later. Raising prices may not sit well with your students. There is a way to offer both a discount to attract people, and still price yourself at the class price you need to succeed. Price your class at the price you need to charge, then offer an introductory discount. That way your price is appealing now, and you don't have to raise the price for students who go on to taking other classes or recommend someone else to your class. After all, raising your class prices when you haven't been in business very long can leave people worrying this may happen again all too soon.

Working at home has a lot of conveniences. However, it doesn't remove the need to run your business in a professional manner. From keeping track of paperwork and customers to using good phone etiquette, you need to present all the polish of a large, well-run corporation. That being said, it will quickly become evident that working from home can leave your clients feeling that you are at their beck and call twenty-four hours a day. Just as you set rules professionally for yourself, you need to structure your work hours so you both serve your customers, and still have a life outside of work.

Keeping Track of Paperwork for Your Clients' Dogs

Creating a paper trail is a term used for a lot of different businesses. That trail can tell you where you began, how you traveled, and where you ended up with anything from money transactions to working with dogs either in private consultations or classes. The purpose of a paper trail is to both help you retrace your steps whenever you need to and help someone else follow your path should you need outside help. Paper trails may also help if someone challenges your credibility or the logic behind the methods you use.

Notes When Doing Private Consultations

The notes you make while doing private consultations are an essential part of your business. Well-constructed notes can help you keep track of small details and keep track of progress. A few key notes can remind you about your train of thought when working with a particular dog, or cue you to look up some additional information for a particular case.

When working with a private consultation, one of the best places to begin your notes is when you first contact the client. Oftentimes that happens over

Preliminary Consultation Notes

How old was the dog when you got him or her? _____

How long have you had the dog? _____

When did you first see problems crop up? _____
_____

Are there other dogs in the household? What is the history with these dogs? _____
_____

When did you get them? _____

How do they add to the main dog's issues? _____
_____

How do other dogs react to the problem? _____
_____

Who else lives in this house or visits on a regular basis? _____
_____

How do the dogs interact with them? _____
_____

the telephone, although jotting notes while you talk can be done, it can also be distracting. What I like to do is make note of the highlights, then ask if the person is willing to e-mail me more detailed information. Above you will find a list of things to include about the dog.

I then like to have a detailed record of the main problem the owner sees in the dog as well as any other issues the owner has concerns about. This all helps me prepare before I arrive to do my canine consultation.

The notes don't stop with this initial data. Notes taken during or shortly after a consultation can help you keep track of subtle issues you may see with the dog. Take a moment to review what you have jotted down about the dog and what work you did with the dog owner. You can use that information to create homework for your client. You will also find that if you leave written homework, the dog owner will be more likely to do any follow-through training. You don't necessarily need to be the one who writes down the homework. Let them do that, then check to see if they fully understood what you want them to do.

In the beginning of your business, you may have to take a moment to jot something down. Be sure to keep a notepad handy to make this easy to do. After doing behavior consultations for a while, you may find that you have trained yourself to better remember small but significant details. It is still a good idea after you leave the client's house and get into your car to take a few moments to jot down information about your visit. You might also want to take along a small tape recorder to record information. Both can help you later when you transcribe the information.

Some of the details that are important to note are how the dog and owner relate. Look for the dog's reaction to the owner when the owner is trying to get the dog to respond to commands. Also study how the owner reacts. For example, if you have a more sensitive dog who also doesn't respect his owner and therefore blows off commands, you need to observe if the owner tenses or becomes angry toward the dog, which can cause the dog to react with unwanted behaviors triggered by the owner. By jotting notes, you can leave the owner with a list of body language cues that may be causing an issue such as submissive urination. Later when you come back as a follow-up, you will know what cues to look for from the dog and owner relationship. You can also make notes of other people in the household. Were they present, and if not, why not? Ages of any children need to be documented as well as other members of the family. Ideally, all of them are present so you can examine how the dog and the family relate to the problem. When doing a follow-up consultation, it is often a good starting place to review the homework list and observe the owner working on that training so you can coach and correct anything that needs a bit of modification.

Another good reason to have good notes is just in case there was an incident where the owners decide to sue you. Although we don't like to think of this kind of a situation, unfortunately these things can happen, justified or not. To help, should this ever happen, be sure to make your notes detailed about whether or not the owner followed any of your instructions. If the dog has failed to improve between consultations, talk to the owner as to how much of their homework was done and make notes assessing what the owner did and didn't do in working to reform the dog's issues.

Oftentimes, when you come to consult on a problem dog, the dog owners are looking at the "tip of the iceberg." They are seeing an issue that has taken time to manifest, and therefore will take time to undo. Don't hesitate to give your client a short list of the future training that the dog will need for reform, and if possible, an estimated timetable to achieve that training. Of course, emphasize that this timetable is only an estimate.

Once you get home be sure to finalize your notes. Make notes of any homework you left, and what level of change you expect by the next time you meet. The busier you become in your business the more important good notes will become.

Consultation Notes

Date: _____

Dog's name, age, breed: _____

_____

Primary complaint: _____

_____

History

    When acquired dog:_____

    When problem occurred: _____

    Previous training history:_____

Family History

    Family members and ages:_____

    How they interact with the problem dog—react to problem: _____

    Other dogs in the household: _____

        When got other dogs: _____

        Age and interactions:_____

        Behavior problems with these dogs: _____

My analysis of issues: _____

_____

How the dog reacted to my training: _____

_____

How the dog reacted to owner trying to do training: _____

_____

Assessment of training session: _____

_____

Recommendations for future training: _____

_____

Homework assigned:_____

_____

Other comments and long-term expectations: _____

_____

Class Syllabus and a Contract for Training Classes

A syllabus is an outline or a summary of the main points for a course of study. Often we don't think of people bringing their dog to a class as undertaking a study, but a good class does fill that need. Just as anyone taking on a class from a college can benefit from a syllabus, so can your students. You will find that many of your students will be highly distracted, especially the first day, with what their dog is doing and what the other dogs are doing. Few have come prepared to jot notes, and even if they did, they probably can't do that effectively in a dog training class. To make sure that your students don't miss some of the important information you present in your class, a syllabus which includes some notes, can be very helpful.

When I do a syllabus, I include information about the training for each session. I find even though I am illustrating training techniques, then observing my students do the training as well as coaching, when the students go home to practice, they can forget some of the finer points. Since I fill my syllabus with class notes, the students' practice session often becomes more effective. I also find that giving out the syllabus tends to make the students more likely to practice in between classes. A class syllabus can help people who, that first day, are wavering about taking this class to realize that there is a lot of important content in the weeks that follow. A Sample Syllabus outline for the first-week class can be found on page 101.

A class contract is important because it puts in writing the requirements for the class. Some classes have age limitations or requirements, while others may have previous training requirements. Unfortunately, you will always find a student here and there who doesn't want to adhere to your requirements. That can cause others in the class to get less value out of the lesson or may even pose a danger to dogs or people. A contract that outlines requirements gives you grounds to dismiss a student without giving a refund. The contract can also provide a signed liability waver and collect contact information. An example of a contract is on page 102.

Listing Class Requirements

On your first day of class, with the exception of some of the higher-level classes, you will often find yourself involved in getting the dog owner squared away with the right kind of equipment, and sometimes teaching them things as simple as how to

Week One

Introduction of instructor and students and puppies.

Check shot records.

Logistics: Where you can and can't park. How to deal with doggy "oops" both inside and outside of the building.

Equipment check.

  Illustrate and discuss good equipment and unacceptable equipment for this class.

  Illustrate and discuss doing a puppy collar check since puppy is growing.

  Illustrate and discuss tags and other identification.

Discuss puppy playtime and social opportunity, and why that is divided into two groups.

Make group assignments.

Show how to correctly feed a treat to prevent mouthing and nipping.

Introduce the bird beak technique.

Talk about good treats and bad treats.

Question and answer session for people about how things are going with potty training.

Talk about crate training.

Field any questions about behavior problems.

Wrap up and remind about coming early for puppy playtime in first group.

Second group, the shy ones, will stay after class for puppy socialization.

Week One Notes:

The bird beak feeding method to prevent mouthing: _____

_____

The basics of housetraining:_____

_____

The basics of crate training: _____

_____

Good and bad treats:_____

_____

Information about correct and incorrect equipment: _____

_____

REMINDERS:

Where to park

How to handle messes outside the building

This is an eight-week course which meets on _____ at _____ p.m. The class begins on _____ with the last class on _____.

Requirements for the Class: Puppies must be between the ages of ten to fourteen weeks on the first day of class. A copy of the dog's shot record showing vaccinations are up to date is required on the first day of class. I realize that vaccinations with puppies are no guarantee the dog is secured from exposure to disease.

Bad Weather: On days when road conditions or weather is questionable, an e-mail will be sent out no later than two hours before class begins. If you have any concerns about the weather or possible cancellation of the class, please contact the instructor by calling XXX-XXXX.

Cancellation Policy. Payment in full is due the first day of class. If the attendee should decide to withdraw from the class on the first day, a refund less a $10 processing fee, will be given. If the attendee withdraws at the end of the second class, half of the class fee shall be refunded. Withdrawal from the class from the third class on shall result in a forfeit of class fee. If the attendee must be removed from the class because of safety or health reasons, no refund shall be offered. There are no refunds for missed classes.

Contact Information
Puppy Name _____ Breed _____ Age _____ Sex _____
Veterinarian Contact Info: _____
Emergency Contact Info: _____
Owner Contact Info (home phone, cell phone, work phone, e-mail): _____
_____
Address: _____
_____
Emergency Contact Info: _____

Liability Waiver
XX Dog Training will endeavor to create as safe an environment as possible for the training. However, I recognize that any dog training is not without risk. Therefore, I agree not to hold responsible XX Dog Training for any unintentional errors, omissions, or incorrect assertions. I agree to abide by the rules of the class and to take responsibility for my dog's actions. Furthermore, I agree to hold harmless XX Dog Training, its officers, directors, instructors, agents, employees, and/or representatives of any and all claims, or claims by any member of my family, or accompanying guests of mine from any injury, expense, costs or damages to myself, my dog, or any handler sponsored by me both for any actions of my dog both in class and out of class. I have read and agree to the liability waiver.

Signature _____ Date _____

correctly adjust a dog collar. You will find it helpful with these classes to send home a list of the correct equipment, as well as some guidelines on how to correctly use the equipment. As well, you can tell them where to get the equipment. If you sell equipment for a class, you can also point that out and tell them that after the class, you can help people with acquiring equipment and for fitting the dog correctly. You may also want to list unacceptable equipment. Many trainers no longer like using slip collars, choke chains, or pinch collars. However, students often show up with these to class. Be sure to give a brief explanation of why you feel these devices are not acceptable.

Certificates of Completion

Certificates of completion are often appreciated by participants in your class. This can be a great way to show that the dog has reached a level of competence in its training. With puppy classes, you often hand these out as a matter of fact. After all, no matter how well the puppy did in the class, that dog can't repeat that course. Because of the dog's age, it must go on to the next level.

In other classes you may want to give out those certificates more judiciously. Some more advanced classes require proof a dog has had a certain level of training. Dogs who have not reached a certain level may need to repeat a class.

Be sure to be tactful when breaking the news to those whose dogs didn't qualify for the certificate. Your students will appreciate you being sensitive to their success as well as you not drawing undue attention to failures. So if you hand out certificates of completion at the end of the class, also hand out certificates of attendance. Don't draw undue attention to the kind of certificate you award, such as giving out all the completion certificates and then handing out the attendance certificates. Instead, mix them up. That way people who need to repeat the class will not stand out. You can use a matter-of-fact tone to explain that people with certificates of completion can go on to certain classes, and people who have certificates of attendance will find value in repeating the class. With some clients, you may want to talk to the people privately if they need to consider private training or a specialized class to help their dog better succeed. After you hand out your certificates, be sure to take the time to tell your students about other classes you offer.

Using the Computer—and More—to Your Advantage

Computers are such wonderful tools. These days, you have a lot more tools available for keeping track of the people who are key to your business. Every day it seems that

apps or computer programs are created to help with everything from organizing key contacts, current clients, past clients, and future clients. Below is a discussion of things to consider when working to help keep track of those you interface with in your business.

Keeping Track of Key Contacts

Contacts can include everyone from students and clients to people you need to deal with for renting a facility. In no time at all, you can find yourself with a pile of contact information. A good way to manage this information is to organize the contacts. One helpful way is to create groups of contact lists. For example, you may have one group designated to collect information about where you hold your classes. In that group, you may include contact for the person you rent the building from as well as utilities and even your insurance agent. In another group, you may keep contact information for any trainers or assistants that help you run the classes. You can create groups by date for people who attend certain classes. After classes are complete you will move people no longer taking your class into your future clients category, because these people are ones you will actively keep informed of events and classes they may want to take. Clients for whom you do private consultations should be in a separate category. Although setting up groups takes a bit of time initially, you save a lot of time when you need to find contact information.

Note: If you need ready access to certain contacts and you have a smartphone or other portable device with Internet access, you may want to enter in key contact information where you can access it remotely. Some of those key people will include contacts for renting and running a facility. That way if you come to teach your class and find the electricity is off, you can work very quickly to resolve the problem.

Keeping in Touch

More than ever before, keeping in electronic touch with people is significant. Not that many years ago, sitting at a computer and accessing the Internet was the primary way people used to reach out and keep in touch. These days, there are a lot of tools for us to keep in touch with the world from smartphones to touch pads. But before you launch into one or more forms of electronic devices, you need to answer a few questions. First, what is your comfort level for learning new technology? If you gobble up this kind of thing, and your budget allows for such a purchase, you may want to look into such a device. But be sure to do your homework ahead of time to discover what kinds of apps are available to suit your business needs. By checking out the apps before you buy a device, you can better decide which device is the better one to buy. If you still struggle using your newest home computer and hesitate to upgrade to newer software, you may want to focus on what you already know to keep in electronic contact with others. After all, starting and running your business will keep you quite busy and you may not have a lot of time to learn the newest technology. However, in the least, you will need to know how to use e-mail to communicate with your clients.

Since in this day and age we all seem to be connected at different levels with technology, don't be surprised to find you will have a mixture of ages and people in your classes, and with that mixture you will find preferences when it comes to communication. So be willing to do everything from handing out computer printouts to e-mailing the people for both your consultations and your regular classes. By being willing to cater to communication at their comfort level, you will find your opportunities for clients may expand.

Keeping Track of Future Clients

Future clients include anyone you talk to who shows an interest in what your business has to offer, as well as anyone who has previously taken a class from you. By keeping track of these clients, you can keep them informed of classes and events you plan on hosting, which will help fill classes. There are a few things to consider with your future clients. One is to try and include information about that particular client's preferences for dog events or needs for training. This way when you send them information, it will be more relevant. If you continually send people things that don't match their interests, they can get into a habit of tossing aside anything you send. So take the time to send them things that have a better chance of catching their interest. To help gather that pertinent information, when a person takes a class from you, take a moment to survey them before they leave. That way you can make notes as to what their interests in dog training or dog events are in the future. If they are someone you met, let's say at a booth you attended at an event, instead of simply talking about yourself and what you do, ask them about their interests with dogs and what kind of dogs they have. Then feel them out for any training interests or training needs. If they have a need you can fill, this is the time to discuss what you can do for them. Ask the person if you can send them information via e-mail or regular mail about classes you have.

The Telephone—Fielding Potential Client Questions

Whether you are offering classes or working with behavior consultations, or both, you can find yourself doing a lot of talking on the phone with potential clients. This can be both a good and bad thing. If you are securing work with your conversation, then that telephone call is well worth your time. However, if you are spending a lot of time talking on the phone, and have no income to show for your efforts, you need to find a way to keep things on point and hopefully land some future income for your effort. Below are some ideas on how to handle telephone communications:

That All-Important First Impression

Your client may be getting his or her first impression of you over the phone. For that reason, you need to come across as the exact person they are looking for to fill their needs. You need to sound calm and confident when talking on the phone. Ideally, you have a way of shutting your office door for these conversations, therefore shutting out any background noises. Even though you are working out of your house, you need to come across as a professional. That means no background dog barking or interference from other members of the household.

Talking Both Professionally and Cordially to Your Clients

When talking to your clients, you have two goals: The first is to come across professionally enough to give them confidence in what you offer, and the second is to come across as someone who is personally there to help them. A good way to get started on this task is to answer the phone with your business name, followed by your name, then ask them how you can help. Have a pad of paper handy for notes. Ask them for their dog's name, the dog's age, and its breed. If this is a breed you happen to be fond of, don't hesitate to mention that. We all like people to think our dogs are great. Likewise, if they happen to have a breed of dog you don't care for, don't lie to them and say you like that breed when you don't. Simply don't make a comment.

Beware that you don't make an unplanned comment by changing your tone of voice. Often when we don't like something, we tend to drop our tone lower and sometimes slow the pace of our words. Be sure not to convey an unwanted message. Keep your tone even and interested.

If the person is looking to attend a class, be sure to have an easy to access list of what all is covered in the class. This way you won't omit telling them the entire contents of the class. By having an outline, you can progress through the information efficiently and in a logical order. Nothing sounds more unprofessional than saying, "oh yeah, I forgot to tell you, we also . . ." That can leave a potential client to worry if you may forget things when you teach the class.

Another thing to have handy to access at a glance is your class schedules. Don't send them to your website to answer this question. That portrays you as too impersonal. Since they have called for information, take a few minutes to answer any specific questions and to assure them that your classes are going to meet their needs. Also, take a moment to discuss the class requirements so you can be sure they are registering for the right class. Close with an invitation to sign them up right then and there. This call to action more often results in a sale than telling them to go to a website to sign up.

If your client is calling about a dog behavior issue, and you do dog consultations, be well prepared to ask specific questions. Dog owners may need to be probed to get to the real heart of the dog's issue and to get them to tell you all the issues. By asking the right questions, you can better decide if this is a case you want to take on. You may want to use some of the questions that reveal the dog's history which are found on the Sample Consultation Notes example on page 99.

Be aware that when you first begin dog consultations, you may need to limit what kind of aggression issues you deal with. Although you may be ready to train a dog not to guard his food bowl, you may not be ready to take on a dog who consistently bites anyone who comes into the house. Don't forget that you will be honing your skills as a dog trainer every day. Although at some time you may be ready to take on the tough challenges, in the beginning, be judicious about working at a level you can find success. After all, your success is what will build your reputation.

At the end of your conversation, you can tell them about your website. Point out what kind of information is waiting there for them to access. Websites are useful tools, and it is great to point them out. But if someone took the time to call, you need to spend a few moments making sure you answer questions they may not have gotten answered at your website.

Keeping the Conversation on Track (Everyone Has a Dog Story)

When you talk to clients, you can easily find yourself spending hours on the phone for which you will not receive any financial compensation. For that reason, you need to learn how to keep a conversation on track. Part of the suggestion of taking down specific history is a good way of interrupting a conversation where the dog owner is beginning to tell you details which are not relevant to the problem at hand. Another way to get the conversation back on track is to learn how to redirect the conversation. Some good redirections include: "That is good information, but more specifically I'd like to ask you . . . ?" If the client still wants to get back to telling you everything that has happened with their dog from the moment they brought it home, you can say, "We can get back to that information later, but for now we need to find out . . ." You may even need to say, "We will cover those kinds of details during the consultation. For now I need to know . . . "

The Great Information Exchange

So far we've discussed the many ways to communicate with potential clients. The one we haven't talked as much about is doing so in person. Trying to think of what to tell a potential client that will convince them that you are the trainer they need

Where to Your Get Your Polish

Writing books on dog training can lead to opportunities for interviews on radio stations. To get ready for my first radio interview, I got some professional coaching from Toastmasters (www.toastmasters.org). Although the name Toastmasters makes people think of giving speeches at a dinner, the wealth of information far exceeds those kinds of speeches. Toastmasters can help anyone in business speak professionally and with confidence. They can also help prepare people like me for radio interviews. Some of their training includes getting better at thinking on your feet when asked questions you weren't expecting. So if you find your skills in communication lacking, consider this option. This is a relatively inexpensive way to gain a lot of professional training from people who have worked through similar communication challenges. And if you are a bit of a wall flower, take heart. Many people who are shy about public speaking go to Toastmasters to conquer that issue, so you will be among people who understand your struggle.

The good news is that you don't have to look very far for a Toastmasters group. This is an international, non-profit organization with many local branches.

is hard to do on the spot when you are face-to-face with someone. A good business owner understands this is a skill he or she needs to hone. To better communicate your strengths and what you can offer, you need to list your qualifications and services, look at what other dog trainers offer, and rehearse communicating your value. That doesn't mean you need to start sounding like someone who reminds you of a car salesman, but you do need to learn how to let people know about your business when you meet them. You may want to begin the conversation by asking the person what they are looking for in a dog trainer, and then work to discover what that customer needs to know from you.

Office Hours—Setting Parameters with Clients and Family

I have gotten into issues with office hours myself. Since I offer support to various rescue organizations via the telephone, and the people involved are located throughout the United States, I've gotten phone calls as early as five in the morning from the East

Coast and as late as ten at night from the West Coast. To help solve this issue, I let people know right away my acceptable hours of operation and my time zone. Never set these kinds of parameters with a negative, "you should know this without being told" attitude. Clients don't know without being told, and they also don't need to be scolded about it. Let's face it. There is a tendency for many clients to think egocentrically. I think we all do this in certain situations. By using a positive manner to set parameters and to deliver the news about what times you can be reached, you will keep your business more manageable. So don't hesitate to take the opportunity to say things like, "And I can be reached by phone between the hours of … " If you have a dedicated answering machine message for your business, use that message to communicate the hours you accept phone calls. All that being said, don't be surprised if you end up needing to call clients in the evening. Because of your client's work hours, you may need to make some compromises.

Explaining Your Business Responsibilities to Your Family Members

Although this may sound a little tongue-in-cheek, you need to train your family members as you would your dog. Instead of expecting them to give you space and expecting them to automatically understand what it takes to run your business out of your home, you need to have a family meeting and discuss each member's roles. Make this interactive, especially if you are dealing with children. Let them express any concerns they have about your time commitments. This may enlighten you to times you need to set aside so the family isn't orphaned by you working out of your home. Make a pact that they will come to you with issues, rather than have them get mad and brood. Explain to them what kinds of things are appropriate to interrupt your work, and what can wait. For things that fall in between an immediate interruption and a need to talk soon, you may work out a knock on the door where they understand you will work to finish up what you are doing and then come to talk to them. Don't be surprised if kids tend to be excessive at interrupting you in the beginning of your business endeavors. Young kids will want reassurance that you'll still be there for them when they want. If you take time to reassure them, this problem will quiet down. So be patient about teaching them to give you the time and space you need. Always make the effort to keep this entire situation positive and supportive.

10

Constructing Your Training Business

The task of constructing your training business will most likely begin at your home. The first step in the process is to gather your thoughts. That task may be done at a kitchen table, or somewhere else you can scatter papers, sort through options, and plot your course. Part of your efforts will be a lot more efficient and accurate because you created a business plan that provides you information about what you need as well as guides your long-term goals. This chapter will help toss out ideas as to different options to consider while at the kitchen table when you make your plans to construct your training area.

Creating Training Areas at Your Residence

Depending upon your business design, you may have the option to create a place in your residence where you can hold classes, or take on dogs to train. If you need a larger area than your residence can accommodate, you may want to rent a facility. Some people will benefit by doing both.

Brainstorming a List

Everyone's dog training business will be unique. For that reason, there is no one list that will fit all dog trainers. Brainstorming is one way you can come up with a list that works for your business. This process involves sitting down in an area where you won't be interrupted, and with pad of paper at hand, jotting down ideas. Sometimes research can help get the brainstorming process started. You may have gathered a bunch of brochures from competitors, or taken an e-tour of other dog training facilities. One of the nice things about the Internet is that your searches can help you gather information from all over the world. Once you get some ideas that intrigue you or look like they may work for your business plan, you can begin the process of sorting the information and categorizing it.

If you are planning on holding classes at your residence, there are a few things to consider. The first is to make sure your homeowner's insurance will allow that decision. The second is to make sure you secure the correct permits and licenses. Once that is out of the way, ask yourself what kind of area do you have to accommodate a class? Will weather be a factor? With those two questions in mind, you might want to take an assessment of your home. Do you have a large enough backyard for outside classes? If you want to work year-round and weather is a factor, do you have an indoor area that can accommodate a class such as an unfinished basement or a garage? If you are using an area with a concrete floor, you will need to put down dog mats. Because of the effort needed to use an indoor area for training in your home, you will probably need to keep that area set up for training in between classes. What that means is that area will no longer be available for family use.

Outside areas seem to be easier to use for both family and for dog training. If you have a large backyard with either dirt or grass, you may find this suitable for a dog class. Even if you need to set up equipment and leave it set up, often this doesn't entirely exclude kids from the backyard. Be aware that if the area has grass, and you have several classes a week, that you may experience wear pattern that kills the grass.

Outside class areas are always susceptible to the weather, but they still may be workable. I've seen outside areas work fairly well in my area. We generally have decent weather for outside events any time from March and April through the end of October. People I've known who have set up outside agility classes have simply limited themselves to the times when weather accommodates their classes. It is a good idea for outside classes to build a containment area. Although chain-link fences can be rather expensive for larger areas, other types of fencing can work as well. By putting up some kind of fence posts, either wooden or metal, and attaching a woven wire, you can create a dog containment fence. This is a good idea should you be dealing with dogs who don't have a recall or who will run off when distracted. The last thing you want is for a critter such as a squirrel to lure a dog away from your class and into harm's way. Even if the situation is that the dog simply needs to be caught after he leaves the training area, this can become an unwelcome interruption to your class.

Getting an Idea of the Size You Need for a Class

Perhaps one of the best ways to determine how large an area you need for a training class is to observe other training classes. Take a look at your local Petsmart or Petco to see how much room they use for different training classes. But don't just stroll by in off-hours. Take time to observe a few classes similar to the ones you plan on teaching. Observe if the area looks effective for the class. Can the students work the dogs like they need, or are they too crowded? When you go to study other dog class areas, take a look at the kinds of instructions. If the instructor merely stands in the middle and lectures or uses a demo dog without letting people practice with their dog, then that area may not be big enough for a class where each dog gets to practice the instruction. Also look to see if the area is large enough to practice a leash walk. I remember one Petsmart instructor who had an area too confined to practice leash walking. He did take the class outside once or twice near the end of the class for a practice. With some classes, the weather just didn't cooperate.

Puppy Classroom Where I Used to Teach

To help you gather your ideas, let me share with you information about a facility I taught at early in my career. These classes were set up by other people in the facility long before I arrived. The puppy class I taught was in a smaller room, about fourteen by twenty feet. Chairs easily fit along the walls. The facility limited the class to ten dogs, but we often had one or two additional family members who accompanied a puppy. The seating area along the walls always seemed large enough to accommodate the extras, but keep in mind that you need more than ten chairs for a class with ten dogs. The area in the center gave me room to not only use a demo dog to illustrate a technique, but to bring a puppy forward and practice with individuals when working to teach sit or down. However, the area was a little small when it came to practicing walking on the leash. Sometimes, if there wasn't a class going on in the larger dog room I could take the class out there and get a better practice with walking on lead. The entire room had dog mats to work on.

The Intermediate Classroom

The second training room at this facility was quite large in comparison to the puppy room, measuring around fifty by seventy feet. When doing the intermediate class, there was plenty of room for students to walk in a large circle when working with dogs who needed to learn good walking manners. Walking as a group makes a big difference when teaching a dog good leash manners it can use outside of the classroom. This larger room was also used for agility and for a class that trained for showing in AKC conformation. There was room to store agility equipment just outside the training area. A portable fence lined the training area. This area also had dog mats. This heated facility was one of many storage unit areas that was rented and converted for commercial use. It seems more and more businesses are converting these kinds of units for business use.

Renting Facilities for Dog Training

I've just talked about the training place where I once taught before I was out on my own. Since this was a facility that had several classes and several trainers, the conversion costs and expense of full-time use as a dog facility was warranted. For someone just beginning in business who isn't using a building for a lot of classes, you may find that the costs for this kind of facility will make it hard to show any kind of profit. Often, when first starting your business, you will need to find somewhere to rent that already accommodates dog training, or can be used for dog training with little additional work.

One idea when looking for a more dog-ready facility is to check out doggy daycare centers in your area. You will most often be giving lessons in the evening or on weekends. Doggy daycares typically accommodate customers during the work week and are not used evenings and weekends. Whatever large area they have for dog play can often be a great dog class area. The place will most likely have restroom facilities for the public as well as a way to deposit doggy doo-doo.

Some veterinarian hospitals have areas large enough to accommodate a training class. You might check with businesses in your area. Once again, they are more likely to have some of the things you need already available that will make doing that class a bit easier, such as a trash can that you can use for any dog messes.

Living in Colorado means it isn't a real long drive to a horse facility. For one of the drop-in agility classes I attended, the training club held classes in a rented indoor horse arena. This worked rather well and, to be honest, some of the shows I went to were held in indoor horse arenas. Often this means you will need a trailer to haul the agility equipment to the arena. With drop-in and higher-level classes, you can often get participants to help set up and take down the equipment, or you can offer a discount to two of the attendees.

Facility Considerations

No matter what place you choose, you need to keep some basic needs in mind. First off, you will need to provide a place where people have access to a restroom. If you are looking into renting a storage unit, keep that in mind. If the storage unit you are looking to rent doesn't have heat or a restroom, then you may find that adding those is very expensive. So if you are looking into renting a storage unit, find one that is already modified to accommodate businesses.

When scouting for a facility, make sure there is enough parking. If you plan on holding classes for ten people, as a minimum, you need to expect ten cars plus one for your car as well as parking should you have an assistant. If more than one class is going on at a time, you will need more parking.

Parking is often paved, although some might be dirt. Keep in mind that pavement is no place for a dog to go potty. Whether you are teaching puppy classes, where dogs need to be walked both before and after classes, or any other kinds of classes, you need somewhere nearby where clients can walk a dog on dirt or grass. If the only thing about a facility that isn't ideal is the doggy doo-doo area, you can use a roll-up piece of artificial grass. But if you do something like that, keep in mind that although dogs will pee in the same place numerous times, they will not poop on top of poop. That means you have to have a decent-size area for the dog as well as keep it cleaned up. So when you go to look at a facility to rent, take a moment to think about both the dog's needs and the student's needs.

Acquiring Needed Equipment

In a start-up business, money is always an issue. So, do your research. If you are holding an agility class, look into equipment you can also sell. More about that idea is discussed in chapter 13. Set up your account with your vendor as soon as possible, and arrange for credit—even if you plan on paying something off when the bill comes. Try to negotiate with the vendor to sell you the equipment at a discount. Let your vendor know that you plan on offering that same equipment for sale at your facility. When it comes to larger equipment that is impractical to keep in stock, don't hesitate to tell all your students, should they like any of the equipment you have, that they can purchase that equipment though you.

Dealing with the Doo-Doo

A few times I've already mentioned about handling doggy doo-doo. There are a few things to keep in mind with this issue. Not only do you need to have a place for the dog to be walked where the dog can eliminate outside, you need to have a place for those eliminations. Having a stock of bags for picking up dog's messes is a good idea. Keep a trash can nearby for those bags to be deposited in. Arrange to have both an inside and outside dog doo-doo can. Use small cans rather than a large one. The biggest reason to use a small trash can is that it is a wise idea not to leave this kind of waste in a trash can very long. People opening up an air-tight trash can that isn't emptied often can quickly become overwhelmed by the odor. This is no way to encourage your clients to deal with their dog's messes. Expect to empty a trash can at least once a day, and if it is hot, do it morning and afternoon. Keep in mind that you need to police areas outside after classes to keep your landlord and neighbors happy. Don't be surprised to find that you end up picking up day-old messes left by some other dog. You need to do this no matter whose dog left behind a mess.

Building Your Reference Library

Your library will vary depending on what you teach or if you only do behavior consultations. Below are some books and video material that can benefit all dog trainers, no matter what they plan on teaching or if they only plan on being a consultant. When you work to build your own library specific to your training, be sure to include books from people who have excelled in your field. In addition, you will need some basic dog training books. Don't hesitate to share recommendations from other dog people when looking to build your library. One thing I think bears mentioning is that some of the older books have some good ideas mixed with ideas that are now becoming obsolete. For example, I was reading a second book by an author who I felt had fairly relevant information years ago when I read him. In his second book, he went on and on about how any and all aggression issues were all rooted in dominance. That concept is quickly becoming outdated. That doesn't mean this book has no value. What it does mean is what I've stated time and time again: This business demands continued learning. And even though you may want to only stock your library with the most recent writing on dog training, you would be well served to also include some of the more dated material.

To illustrate that point, let me tell you about a learning situation that happened to me. Many years ago I read *The Dog's Mind* by Bruce Fogle and Anne B. Wilson. Although in general the book has some good information, nothing really stuck out for me. Now before you dismiss reading this book for yourself, keep in mind that when you read a lot of books, especially close together, you often see repetitions. Some books will simply confirm ideas you have and others will help supply you with information you will use at a later time. And even though this is not a recent book, it does merit reading. In fact, recently I ran across this book collecting dust on my shelf. I was waiting for the arrival of a friend and randomly flipped open the book and began to read spots here and there about aggression. (You will probably be well served to highlight in yellow any book you keep for reference.) In this book, it didn't take long before I read something that really struck a chord. Sure, I'd read that years ago, but that particular bit of information didn't have any reference to me at the time, and didn't stick with me, not even when I encountered such a case years later. Now I saw the reason behind a very difficult fear aggression case I'd come to know intimately. I'll share that experience and see if you can isolate the cause behind this very severe case of fear aggression.

I had helped in raising a litter of Jack Russell Terriers. The mother had quit producing milk when the pups were two days old. These pups needed to be bottle fed to survive. Now that statement may leave you thinking that after our vet visit, where we purchased powdered milk supplement and very small bottles, all we had to do was read the handout the vet gave us on how to nurse very young puppies. After all, that how to nurse very young pups article was written by another vet. I read, and re-read and closely followed everything that was written. The bottle feeding wasn't working. Sometimes the pups would eat, and other times they wouldn't. After a day and a half, I realized I was losing an entire litter of five puppies. Fortunately, I quickly found a woman who'd learned techniques in nursing newborn kittens. She had techniques not mentioned in the vet's article that helped me save the litter. (I wrote about this and the article was published in *Dog World*.)

The day the cat woman came to teach me successful bottle feeding, she flagged one particular puppy as a great concern. That one female was so thin the cat woman worried if the pup could pull through. The puppy did live and we named her Alexis. Since my daughter kept Alexis, I can attest to the fact that we did more than the usual amount of socialization with this dog as a puppy. We continued to work on Alexis's socialization for years with very little progress. It puzzled me why this dog failed to make progress with socialization even though we addressed it day after day and year after year, as well as why she had such a severe level of fear aggression. (I wrote an article about Alexis which received a DWAA nomination. The article was called "Shy or Abused." You can read it on my website. The article was written before my epiphany below.)

I made the effort to check on some of the other members of the litter. It seemed that most of the litter was shyer, even though both parents were anything but shy. Still, none were as extreme as Alexis. After years of looking for reasons, the best conclusion I found was offered by a few veteran breeders who said that perhaps this particular cross created the problem. But that was not the right conclusion. I found the reason a few years after we lost Alexis when I was randomly re-reading *The Dog's Mind* while waiting for a friend. Fogle talked about fear aggression and the association of a young puppy being undernourished. Bingo. We had our reason for the extreme behavior in our beloved dog, a behavior that seemed to defy all attempts to change.

So here is the moral: Although you can expect to read all throughout your career, and expect to go to seminars to harvest other trainers' great discoveries, there are reasons for some books to be on your reference shelf. One is because your initial reading will help give you understanding of dogs and training. The other is that until you have some solid dog experience, some of the information will not stay with you.

Although any information can become dated, I do have a few books or reference materials that I feel belong in your toolbox of information no matter what kind of training you undertake. These, at least for me, seem to ring a true tone on the journey to understanding and working to manage dog behaviors. I've listed them below.

Clicker Training

In the book *Don't Shoot the Dog,* Karen Pryor not only launched many dog trainers into using clickers for training, she probably did the most to begin the conversion from "yank and spank" techniques to a more scientific approach. This is a worthwhile book for any dog training discipline. Use this book as a starting point, but not an ending point.

Her book, *Reaching the Dog's Mind, Clicker Training and What It Teaches Us about All Animals,* is yet another to add to your collection. But I'd also recommend you look into videos that do a good job illustrating how clickers can be used for shaping different behaviors. Years ago, I remember watching a clicker video by Gary Wilkes. The video was so old it was a VHS tape. The video showed how a clicker was used to teach a rambunctious puppy to lie down. You also had the opportunity to watch how to shape a behavior. The video also had a hidden message: Employ the puppy's mind, and you will more quickly wear out the rambunctious pup. I think all dog trainers need to learn how to do clicker training, even if you don't want to use this technique as your core way of managing dog behavior. I don't use clicker training very often, but have done so in a few situations. It certainly has its place in dog training.

Canine Signals

Dog trainers work very hard to communicate to dogs what they want that dog to do. Dogs are working hard to communicate to us. The book *Calming Signals,* by Turid Rugaas, is a great book to educate people about the body language dogs use to communicate (get her updated version, 2005, not the original). This is one of many references you will need when learning to understand what a dog is saying to you or to another dog. Even if you are teaching a puppy class, you need to learn how to detect "this lesson is too much for me to handle, I need to stop here" signals from your canine participants. There are other books you will find on canine body language that you will probably add to your bookshelves. What I found that helped me was when watching dog trainers on television—since I'm not in the thick of the training—to observe how the dog reacts to what the trainer is doing. So do your book learning on canine signals and practice, practice, practice.

Tellington TTouch

I was first introduced to this kind of technique with horses. I had the unfortunate experience of training a horse who didn't, to put it politely, have all of her neurons connected. Unlike normal horses, this horse reacted stressfully to almost everything in her environment. Trying to make an animal with mental training challenges into a ridable horse, even when using ideal techniques, can take years.

One tool I found very useful was the Linda Tellington-Jones video on the Tellington TTouch for horses.

Of course when she came out with a video on dogs, I was eager to view it. Keep in mind that Linda has been heavily criticized on the quality of her videos, though I'd still recommend watching them. She also has a lot of books out, all of which I have on my to-read list. You might check into some of those. There are people who give clinics on this technique. Should one come to your neighborhood, consider attending. I recently attended one and found it helped confirm I was on the right track with some of her techniques I was using, as well as adding some other "touches" to my portfolio. The instructor also covered wraps, which can greatly help some stressed animals.

You may be asking yourself at this point, "Why all the fuss about stress? I plan on doing training classes, not private consultation (at least for now)." What you may not realize is just how easy it is to create stress. In one particular class where I was not the lead agility instructor, I realized the guy teaching was pushing the dogs too far and causing stress, which can be extremely damaging. Stress in training is something every instructor needs to better understand. Ironically, the person who first flagged

Dr. Ian Dunbar

Dr. Dunbar was an early read in my dog training career. At the time, his idea of not being brutal with your training techniques was revolutionary and he offered many techniques that still support the more positive-based training we see today. I found his concept of the redirect something that can be used with many problematic dog behaviors. The basic "golden" message Dunbar had with this technique is if you refocus the dog, you refocus the actions. The redirect is a great tool with a lot of aggression issues.

Last year I had the pleasure of attending his clinic when he gave one in my area. I so wished I'd had that clinic early in my career. He has a wealth of information from great ways to construct puppy classes to dealing with aggression. The good news is that you don't need to attend his lectures especially since he is winding down on doing them. He has many on CD and in books that you can purchase. This allows you to listen and revisit his information. No matter what kind of training you do, he is a must to study.

this issue was Pavlov. He created so much stress in some dogs he was working with that the dogs developed a neurosis. And guess what? He didn't do it while offering punishment. He did it with rewards. His dogs were given rewards when one bell was rung, but not when a different bell tone sounded. Pavlov then began to change those bell tones until they became so close together the dogs couldn't tell when they'd get rewarded and when the tone meant no reward. The dogs broke down mentally. What this means is that people who misuse positive training techniques can really trash a dog's mind if they don't thoroughly understand what they are doing. As a dog trainer you will be well served to look for signs that a dog is saturating out with a lesson. And if you come across a dog that has suffered from excessive stress, keep in mind that wraps and TTouch can be very helpful when working with over-stressed dogs, no matter what stressed out the dog.

These suggestions are only a beginning for your dog training reference library. Keep in mind you will find numerous other trainers, books, and techniques to borrow or adopt techniques from, which may be scattered in bits and pieces amidst information they have to offer. Depending on what your training specialty or specialties are, you will add different things to your library. For example, if you are teaching agility, you will probably have a subscription to *Clean Run Magazine*. If you are teaching Rally, you will probably have a copy of Janice Dearth's book, *The Rally Course Book: A Guide to AKC Rally Courses*. If you are training people to compete in any AKC classes, you will need AKC rulebooks on your shelf as well.

Dressing the Part When Meeting the Public

Dress codes certainly reflect our times. Not to bore you with times gone by, but in my senior year of high school, girls were finally allowed to wear pants to school instead of dresses. No, I didn't attend a private school or religious school, mine was just an ordinary public secondary school.

Of course, we were not allowed to wear any blue jeans. Things have certainly changed. All that being said, you need to look in the mirror before you head out to teach a class or go on a dog consultation. Although blue jeans may be fine, make sure they are not worn or have dirty areas. Likewise, make sure your shirt or blouse is neat and fits you well. And although you don't need to dress like a nun or a priest, don't wear anything that is the least bit provocative. Keep in mind that what you dress in becomes your calling card to the public. Your clothes make a first impression, and for some people if you make the wrong impression, you will spend time reclaiming the respect that mistake cost you. So work to look neat and tidy, and dress a little better than the participants in your class.

Dog Consultations

About fifteen years ago, when I began my dog consultation part of the business, someone brought me a German shepherd with aggression issues. At the time, I didn't have a lot of experience working with different kinds of aggression. After my first session with the people, I realized I didn't have the skills needed to deal with this dog and told the owners they needed to find a different trainer. Unfortunately, with the extreme issues this dog had, after they worked with two different trainers and spent in excess of a thousand dollars, the dog was still dangerous. For the safety of their family and others, they elected to euthanize the dog. Since that time I have done a lot to hone my skills when dealing with aggression.

Recently, I took on two fear-aggressive dogs that other trainers had failed in reforming. Both were rated as class-five aggression. I managed to reform both dogs and both were adopted as pets. The point I wish to make has been said before in a different way. As a dog trainer, you will learn throughout your career. But what also needs to be said is that there is no shame at any time in your career if you turn down a job, because you feel you can't improve the dog. For some dog trainers, taking on more severe aggression cases will never be part of their business, and that is just fine. For others, like me, they will first need to gather a certain level of skills before taking on those kinds of dogs.

On that note, when doing dog consultations more than just the dog comes into play. I had one client I tried to work with to resolve her dog's aggression. Solving the dog's issues wasn't the problem; the owner was the issue. Finding that this person seemed unwilling to follow my guidance, as a last ditch effort, I referred this person to another dog trainer well skilled in canine aggression issues. My hope was that after two people told her what she needed to do, she'd actually take action. After two sessions I got a call from the other trainer. She was also frustrated with working with this client who would follow none of her instructions. Since that event, I have learned rather than frustrate myself, if I get strong vibrations that the dog owner isn't going to do anything to help out the dog, I pass on that client. In all honesty, these kinds of people, especially when working with aggression issues, can end up getting you hurt. That being said, I have found most clients have good intentions and will work to help solve their dog's problems. Some will go to great lengths for the benefit of their dog.

I also had the experience with a dog customer where they had a dog they left under my care for three weeks. I expected this board-and-train situation to be more about boarding than training since they only mentioned minor issues they were having with the dog. But the dog had a major issue I discovered after a few days. He could be triggered into submissively peeing, and once you triggered him, all be it unintended, he was relentless. I found myself unable to solve the issue using the normal techniques, so I called a host of other dog trainers in hopes of finding a solution to this issue. None of my resources had any ideas. Finally, I came up with something unique to try and found success. I wrote about that technique and the article won an award from the DWAA.

The point I am getting at in all of this, is that when you begin your dog consultation business, you will need to decide what kinds of behavior issues you will and will not take on. Make sure you structure your efforts toward areas where you can have success. Remember that you are building a reputation as you go. Also remember that you are also building your education. So even if you can't handle a dog situation now, take on more studies and perhaps you will be able to manage it in the future. By the same token, there will be a balancing act where you find a dog issue you don't know how to solve, but with a lot of research and some perseverance, you may find success and have a breakthrough in your learning.

Creating a Training Contract

Having a good contract with your client can create a safety net for you. In your contract, have a section that includes information about your client and the dog. Include breed information, age, gender, and overall health. Give them room to list any health issues, any medications, and any food allergies. Have an area that tells what kind of service you are providing. Provide an area where they can list any serious behavior issues such as biting. You may be well served to suggest certain things by providing a list of issues. Finally, you will need an area where they will sign, which becomes your liability waiver. This will protect you in the event of an accident or injury to animals or people. After you draft your contract, you may be well served to run the paper by a legal professional.

Use a contract with all your clients. If you stop service with a client for a significant period of time, and the client wants to again do training, consider doing a new assessment and a new contract. Make sure to get all signatures and all areas filled out, then file that contract where you can find it if you need to. You will find a Sample Boarding for Training Contract on page 124.

Date: _____

Dog's name, breed, and age: _____

Identification (please circle):   Tags   Microchipped   Identification collar

Other: _____

Veterinary contact info: _____

Please notify your vet that the dog will be under my care during the training time frame and get permission for me to seek treatment if needed. I will first try to notify you, but please give the vet parameters for treatment and dollar amounts you are willing to pay for your dog. Please briefly state those parameters below. Dog shots must be up to date. Please send a copy of the rabies vaccination—can be faxed to me or e-mailed.

Your contact info (cell, home, work, e-mail): _____

Name and contact info for a relative or friend who can make decisions in your absence: _____

Feeding: Please supply dog food for your dog. State feeding schedule and amount of food. Please state what kinds of treats your dog gets and responds well to. _____

Food issues, medical issues: Please note any food issues (for example, if the dog reacts poorly to higher fat treats or any preservatives in treats). Please state any medical issues the dog has or may be susceptible to, such as bloat. Give approximate dog weight: _____

Training: I am leaving my dog for training beginning _____ and ending _____

Fees:

Boarding: $_____ a day (owner provides food and supplements).

Training fee: $_____ a day. Half payment due when dropped off. Payment in full when the dog is picked up.

I understand that the dog will be worked at least once a day on training issues. The dog may be worked both on and off the property and helpers may work with the dog. I also understand that on the day I pick up the dog I will be offered a lesson with the dog to help transfer the training. On back of this contract, I have listed my major concerns with the dog. I understand that some issues take time to change, and that an ongoing effort to maintain improvement will be necessary on my part. I also understand that while under the trainer's care, sometime unexpected accidents can happen. I do not hold the trainer responsible for injury or death to my dog, or my dog's actions. The trainer agrees to conduct training and care with efforts to avoid any such occurrences.

Signature of Owner: _____

11

Marketing and Public Relations

Advertising. It's everywhere—on your television, on the radio, in your newspaper, magazines, and arriving all the time in your mailbox. Running ads is one way to do marketing, and marketing is the way people learn about your business. After all, there is no way to have a successful business unless people know about you. For most home-based dog training businesses, marketing will make or break them. And although that means it is worthwhile to set aside money for marketing, if those dollars don't produce income, you won't build your business.

Building Word of Mouth

Word of mouth is often cited as one of the most powerful advertising tools you can have. The best part about this kind of marketing is that you don't pay anyone to spread the good word. Happy customers love to tell about their experience. To create a happy customer you need to have a customer-pleasing product. The other thing you need is customers to please. Unfortunately, when you are first starting off this may seem like you are chasing your tail. You need to have happy clients to have good word of mouth, but without some kind of marketing you can't build word of mouth.

One way to begin to build word of mouth before you have regular clients is to offer a sample dog training session free of charge. Perhaps you can arrange this though an area veterinarian. You can show people how to deal with a common issue or two such as standing still on the weighing stand at the vet's office and how to introduce their dog to brushing teeth. Have the vet help promote the event by giving out flyers to customers in advance. If the vet has a newsletter that he or she e-mails, ask to have that information included. Be ready to hand out little information packets about your classes or other services you can offer the attendees. When you tell them of your services, just announce the advantage, but don't push. However, do make it very convenient for them to sign up. You may query the vet as to what kinds of manner issues he or she sees most often so you can design one of your classes around solving those issues. Once you get your clients in the door with a short and easy class to resolve their most annoying problem, you can work to enlighten them about other classes you offer and how they can make their dog more pleasant to live with. If you simply want to deal with behavior issues through consultations, a class such as this can bring to light issues some of your clients have with their dogs that you can help solve with a one-on-one consultation.

Websites That Sell Your Business

These days, phone books are collecting dust because when people want to find a phone number, they often do an online search. Let's face it. The Internet has become vital to most people's lives. For that reason, you need to have a web presence. There are a lot of options when looking to create a website. Some companies offer relatively inexpensive software to help you create your own website. There are a host of web designers available. Cost is always a factor to consider. Although this is a very important part of your business, you need to keep the costs reasonable. If you are hiring someone to do your website, be sure to thoroughly check out other work they have done. Also agree on initial design costs as well as updates to your website. Updates can help keep your site more appealing and help you to keep information about current classes easy for people to view.

Using Social Media

People regularly use various social media to reach out to others. You may find using either Facebook, Twitter, or YouTube can help to capture new customers for you. Below is some information about these popular social media opportunities.

Facebook

Facebook reaches out to the entire world. This medium is often used to get groups of people together, from a family reunion to a high school reunion. Facebook can be used to pass along messages or opinions to different people. A dog person may post something like "Went to my agility show today, and got a second leg in open jumpers. Just one more to go." Someone else may post on your site a response such as "Great

An Insider's Perspective on Web Design

Tia Olson is the web designer I use. She recently received her Masters of Engineering in Computer Science, which included a user-centered design course. She has ten-plus years' experience in web page design. Below is her information about the ins and outs of websites.

To have a successful business, you will need a website. The first step is addressing the infrastructure, (discussed in chapter 4) which includes securing a website address and web server. There are a lot of options when looking to create a website. Some of the options include hiring a professional designer to build the website, using licensed software products to build and design the website yourself, or using freeware software to build and design.

If you are looking to do it yourself, you will find that some companies offer relatively inexpensive software packages for hosting your website and building your website. If you are looking to hire someone, there are a host of web designers available anywhere from high schoolers to professionals with advertising degrees and huge portfolios of success stories. Cost is always a factor to consider. Although this is a very important part of your business, you need to keep the costs reasonable. If you are hiring someone to do your website, be sure to thoroughly check out other work they have done. Before writing that first check, get in writing how much they will charge for the initial design costs, as well as updates to your website. Updates can help keep your site more appealing and help you to keep information about current classes easy for people to view. Ultimately, even if you decide to have your website done by someone else, the responsibility for the effectiveness of this as an advertising and marketing tool still falls on your shoulders.

Your initial message will be contained on your home page. Make sure that page portrays the right message. Your mission is to communicate that your potential customer has arrived at a professional dog training business. At a glance, anyone looking at your home page should be able to know this site is about dogs. But don't get cute. This is not the place for humor or trying to make people go "ah" about some kind of personal moment. Nor is this a place for you to dazzle with graphics in motion. Keep in mind that people who search out your website will be looking for information. Make that readily available for them to secure.

Keep in mind that your website is there to inform. There are two kinds of information you need to contain on your website: The first is all about your business. You need to answer the how, what, when, where, and why. Tell them how you can help them with dog issues, what you offer, when you hold classes, where you are located, and why they need to sign up with you.

The second kind of information tells the visitor that this website gives them something they can use. Although some people will simply come to the website because you already let them know this is where to go to find out about your great classes, others may be looking to solve behavior issues. If you give them some information to help them understand their dog issues, you can sometimes guide them to a class you offer which can help them resolve their dog issues.

Keep your website updated. There is nothing more frustrating than going to a website to check into the next class available only to find that class isn't yet posted. All you can see is old information. Websites that have old information can leave the customer wondering if the business is going to remain open or if it is in decline and going to close.

Findability is very important to any website. Although you won't list all your information details on your home page, you need to make sure that people visiting your website can find and click to the information details they need from your home page. You need to make finding information as easy as possible, especially when that information means securing a sale. So be sure people can access both class description from the home page as well as class schedules. It is a mistake to ask a website visitor to have to click on the class description before they can get to the class schedule.

Don't bog down your home web page with heavy-loading factors. A checklist of items that slows down a website includes high-resolution and large graphics. Music and video will also slow down loading of content. Although these items may tempt you to put them on your website, you really don't need them to sell a dog business.

Make that website easy to read. Tiny type can frustrate users. So can white text on black background. Red text can also be challenging. Stick to what is easy to read. If you are looking for a good guide to the frustration factor with this, find someone in their fifties and ask them to give you feedback as to how visually challenging the text is to them.

Be well organized. People expect to find a navigation and menu bar where they can easily click to navigate the website. Put your clickable information in a logical place and make sure the font size isn't too small. Make sure that it also contains common controls like a home button/link both at the top and bottom (or sides) along with contact information. If you have login/logout abilities make sure they are easy to find.

Lastly, make sure you don't have typos on the page. If you or your website designer aren't good at catching these, have someone help (perhaps a family member) who can help proofread.

In General

- Ensure visibility from remote devices—most simple websites can be viewed from phones but check your website from all sorts of devices to make sure it works.

- There are many free and reasonably priced tools for web designing/creating/tools; you don't need to re-invent the wheel. For example, don't try to create shopping cart solutions and built-in calendars.

- Technology is constantly changing. Try to ensure you keep up but be wary of constantly jumping to the next best fad as the cost/time may not be worth it.

- Depending on the type of dog business you are going for, like agility training, try to join newsletters and groups associated with your business so you can add information to your website such as a local, upcoming dog trials.

- Hook into other web options like Twitter, Facebook, Google+, and YouTube. Remember to read the license agreements and so forth to ensure you are not in any violations.

- Take advantage of the articles and books that inform you how to drive people to your website when it is hidden among millions of others. Decide what makes sense for the level of your website, things like linking to other local businesses' websites.

- Remember that people will do Internet searches based on your name and your business name, so keep those personal web search results in mind. Find out what is needed for Google or other search engines to recognize your company as a dog business near your location so when people do Internet searches for "dog businesses" in your area it comes up correctly.

As your company grows so should your website. Start simple and expand. Get feedback from customers and compare to what others are doing. Many web services allow you to track statistics to help you monitor what methods help increase your business.

job." That is, of course, provided you have set up your Facebook page as open instead of private. There are two things that Facebook can be useful for to you as a business owner. One is that you can use it to post news and events. And the other is that you can post information about your business, much like an advertisement.

If you decide to do a Facebook page, or a similar kind of social network, be sure to post great dog pictures and work to make dog searches land on your page. If you do have people asking to be "your friend," do more than click the accept key. Reach out to these people. Find out about their dogs, their dog interests, and query about their dog needs. If you build a relationship with each fan, they'll become a fan and a customer forever.

Some businesses use incentives to get people to visit their page by inviting them to "like" their Facebook page to receive a 50 percent off coupon, etc. "Likes" help others find your business. You can view other Facebook pages your friends like, your page will appear in the "Likes and Interests" section of the user's profile, and you have the ability to publish updates to the user. Your page will show up in the same places Facebook pages show up around the site, and you can target ads to people who like your content.

Consider using the Facebook blog to talk about common issues seen with dogs that you help resolve in your class. You might want to do a short "case study" each week or month. Just be sure to keep the identity of your student and dog private. When working through a medium like Facebook, you will not see an instantaneous return. You need to look at this as a long-term opportunity for people to get to know about you as a dog trainer. Keep in mind that Facebook is more about relationships than business. That being said, it can also be a way for people to get to know you better. And don't we all prefer to take a class from someone we know something about?

Facebook can be used as a cheap (free) website for your business. In addition to setting up an independent website, you may investigate setting up a Facebook page and put in your fliers and business cards.

YouTube

Previously, I talked about how one way to gain customers may be to give a short training demo for free through your local vet's office. Another way you can introduce yourself and show people a little bit about how your dog training can help them is by doing a short YouTube video. Although YouTube reaches out to the world, it can be just as valuable when working to find local customers.

Think through your video clip. This is going to be like a commercial where you have a few minutes instead of thirty seconds to capture your audience and get across a message. You may want to show a clip that illustrates part of a training class, with more of an emphasis on showing the results of your training. If you offer agility classes, you may want to show short clips of dogs beginning to learn agility followed by how much fun the dog and owner are having during and after taking your class. Although YouTube videos are open to the world, you can use them as part of the information at your website. If you use a YouTube video in this way, have an area on your website that clearly tells viewers that they can click to the video to learn more about your classes.

YouTube videos should not be very long. Although the time limit is fifteen min-
utes, you should be able to get a strong message across in less than five minutes. Your purpose should be to show them something they can use, and inform them of other training they maybe didn't realize they needed, as well as tell them how your classes can offer them the canine training solutions they need. You can then refer them to your website for more information. At your website, you will want to include a link to your YouTube videos.

Should You Be on Twitter?

In 2011, Twitter had one hundred million active users logging in at least once a month and fifty million active users every day. Wow! And all you need is about ten people per class. So can Twitter help you make your numbers? Do you need to learn how to Tweet and spend your time with this medium? Twitter has been used for a variety of purposes in many different industries. However, this is more of an interactive and social interface that can be likened to a "virtual watercooler."

Twitter gets hits with what is called a Twitter tag. For this to work for a dog business, you'd create a specific tag that identifies you. That tag needs to be fairly unique

and have a high interest level to draw people to you. Celebrities, news stations, and even some politicians have the right kind of pull. In general, people on Twitter are looking for tweets about things they are following from a news angle or socially. For marketing to the public, your time and efforts with this medium will most likely not gain a lot of clients. What Twitter is best for is to allow you to follow updates from your friends, industry experts, favorite celebrities, and what's happening around the world. Tweeting is more about the moment than about a dog class next week.

Blogging

The term *blogging* was coined in the early 1990s. Soon what began as an online journal became touted as the newest and greatest marketing tool. Everyone from authors to major corporations were blogging. The high hopes of marketing success through blogging have waned. If you want to use this as a marketing tool, you need to do so strategically or you may find, like many corporations did, that this is a waste of time. If you decide to do a blog, keep in mind that this is more a tool for the world than local people so you need to find a way to motivate local people to read your blog. If you are blogging about a puppy class, most of those people will not be out on the web looking for information. However, if you have a drop-in agility class, you may be able to encourage your students to check your blog. If you keep them up to date with happenings in the class and how people are finding success with some of the techniques you use, you can keep them motivated to attend your class and you may even snag some new people. You may want to tell them if you recently attended an agility clinic and how excited you are to cover your new training discoveries in class. Agility people and more advanced dog training class candidates are more likely to be out looking for info and therefore more likely to stumble across your blog. Although there are several places you can blog, the best place to do so is on your website.

Business Cards and Brochures

With the ease of today's computers, you can make both your business cards and brochures at your desk. It can certainly save you some money to do this, as long as you do it well. On your business card, realize that the goal is to give people something that quickly communicates who you are, what you do, and how to get ahold of you. Use your logo! Try and fit in some kind of dog picture because a picture is worth a lot of words. Have your name and phone number easy to read, and include your e-mail

Google AdWords

AdWords is Google's paid advertising product. When someone types in a Google search for a subject such as dog aggression, little ads appear at the top, sides, and sometimes bottom of the search. Those ads can become a promotional tool for your business. The advantage to this ad is that you are not charged for the appearance of your clickable ad, you are only charged should someone click through to your website. You determine the cost of the ad by bidding. The person who bids the most gets a better position when ads appear. Fortunately, if you've set a maximum CPC (Cost Per Click) bid of $1 for your ad, and if your competition bids only $0.50 for the same ad position, you'll only need to pay $0.51 to show your ad, assuming your ads are similar in all other aspects.

For some this may seem like a good way to help out their business. After all, you're charged only if someone clicks on your ad and lands on your website, not when your ad is displayed. But a few dog trainers I've talked to didn't feel this worked well for them. To have this advertisement work well, you need to have a talent for capturing a person's interest and motivate them to take a look at your website in the allowed characters: twenty-five in the headline, thirty-five each in the two lines of text and thirty-five in the display URL. Once they arrive at the website you need to find a way to get them interested in your training product. If you decide to try AdWords, expect to put some work into the project and be willing to learn. After your campaign is set up effectively, keep monitoring it to find out what's working and what's not.

and/or website. If your business name doesn't tell clearly what service you offer, include a brief statement about that.

When doing a brochure, make sure those picking it up know immediately what that brochure is all about. Again, a good picture can often say a lot as well as attract a lot of attention. Your brochure needs to quickly communicate what you have to offer; however, unlike a business card, you can get into more detail. What you don't want to do is to become as dry as a textbook when trying to communicate to your prospective client. What you do want to do is catch their attention, sometimes by mentioning a problem they may be struggling with, then tell them enough to let them know you are the answer to their problem. Make sure your brochure looks professional and is edited. Typos and amateur-looking pamphlets send a message you don't want potential clients to see. See Appendix D for an example.

Advertising through Veterinarians, Groomers, and Doggy Day Care Centers

Not everyone cares about your services, especially if they don't have a dog. So it only makes sense to focus your advertising to where people who have dogs typically go to spend money on those dogs. Three places you need to include in your advertising efforts are veterinarians, groomers, and doggy day care centers.

Check with veterinarians in your area and see if they have a bulletin board for posting dog information. Some veterinarians allow trainers to set out small advertisements for training services. Everything from a small color brochure to your business cards can be displayed in a clear plastic rack. If you go this route, be sure to make that brochure effective and eye-appealing. If they have a monthly newsletter, you may ask if you can include short training tips. In your credentials listed at the end of the piece, you can mention your business.

Don't just set out the advertisement and run out the door. Take a few moments to talk to the front office help. Ask them about their dogs and their dog interests. Tell them about the kinds of services you offer in a conversational way. This will make them more likely to point out your services should a client inquire. If it is possible to talk to the veterinarian or veterinarians at the office, take that opportunity. Introduce yourself, be friendly but businesslike. Tell them ways you may be able to help their clients. Show them where you've left your information so if they decide to pass along your name, they will know just which information to direct their client to.

Talk to local groomers. These people often have to deal with problematic dogs. Do some friendly dog talk by asking about some of their most difficult dogs. Tell them what services you offer and ask if you can include some information for their clients. Ask the groomer if you can put out some flyers at their shop, and offer to pass along information about their business in exchange. You can tell the groomer that you will offer a discount to the customers they refer for trying out your services.

Get to know your local doggy day care centers. Ask them if they have clients who are having particular problems. One doggy day care had some owners whose dogs peed every time they came to pick the dog up. If you can help resolve a problem like this, ask the doggy day care to refer you to the customer and leave information so the dog owner can get in touch with you. See if the doggy day care has a bulletin board for posting your information or if they will let you put out a rack with flyers or business cards. But don't just drop off information. Take a little time to talk with the employees at these places so you can tell them what kinds of dog classes you teach or what kinds of dog training you offer. This can help generate word-of-mouth advertising. If the center has a newsletter, see if they will let you include short tips for dog management and training.

Advertising through Print

Dog Magazines

Placing an advertisement in *Dog World* will most likely not gain you a single customer for your dog training business. National magazines just have too broad a customer base, and the cost for their ads reflects that coverage. However, you may find you will have better luck if you place an ad in a more local magazine. Go online and see if there are any local dog magazines. In my area, there are a few. One is called *Mile High Dogs*. A second magazine is called *Petacular* that is distributed for free at doggy businesses and veterinarian offices. Both magazines cater to the local population and are a better kind of magazine in which to consider placing an ad.

Another place to find a more locally oriented magazine is a veterinarian office. Some vet offices carry animal content magazines. Although some of these magazines are published nationally, you may check to see if they accept local ads, meaning they print different ads for each region where they distribute.

If you have writing skills, check with any local magazines to see if they'd accept a dog training article. I've done that for both of my local dog magazines and have obtained clients who called me after reading my articles.

Local Ads

Newspapers used to be king when it came to advertisements. That is no longer true. For dog trainers and dog training, ads in a newspaper aren't going to reach the right audience very often, and for that reason may not be a good place to spend your advertising money.

Yellow Pages in Your Local Phone Book

At one time, if you wanted to find a local business, you grabbed a phone book and flipped to the back to the yellow pages. Mixed in with the lists of phone numbers were boxed-out advertisements for some of the businesses, so you could get a better idea which one to choose. The yellow pages in our area has grown so large that they are contained in a separate book. The usefulness of yellow pages for the average customer is changing. For dog trainers, this kind of advertising will most often not be money well spent. More and more people do phone number searches online. There, they can get more content than even a very expensive ad in the yellow pages will provide them.

Dog Booths at Shows or Events

Some of the advertisement suggestions thus far have talked about going to where your customers aggregate, such as veterinarian offices and doggy day care centers. But sometimes it is nice to have doggy people come to you. A way to do this is at a dog event that hosts booths.

There are several events that have this opportunity in my area. Some are associated with dog shows such as an AKC show. Others have been hosted by rescues to help raise money. All of them have one thing in common: They are all about dogs and dog people.

One I have gone to a few times in my area is called Bark at Briargate. At this annual event, rescues as well as a variety of dog vendors set up their booths. You can have packets of material to hand out as well as the opportunity to meet and talk to a lot of people. A couple of things to consider if you are doing a booth:

- You need something free to give out. You can put dog treats in an information package to hand out. You can set out dog treats.
- Since you will find other dog trainers also have booths set up, to stand out you may want to give a demonstration every half hour.
- Try to bring some of your family support along so you can have a break and be able to go around to other booths to do a bit of networking.
- Be sure to have a lot of business cards to hand out.

Mailing Out Advertisements

A business-size envelope just arrived in my mail the other day. Inside were slips of paper advertising different businesses. Perhaps you've gotten one of these in the mail or perhaps you got a glossy postcard advertising anything from steam cleaning your carpet to tires and an oil change. With all those people who have dogs in need of training, this may be a tempting way to communicate to them that your services are at the ready. However, this type of advertisement may not be the best for your fledgling business. First off, the card needs to be designed to catch the customer's eyes and deliver your message of how your services can benefit them while using very few words. Typically the most effective cards are designed by a professional. Professional designs can be expensive. Likewise, mailing out cards is expensive from postage to the costs of printing the cards. Lastly, for this type of advertising to work best, you must rely on exposure to help sell your services. That means one mailing won't get you a great response, but mailing on a quarterly basis for a year or two will get you a better response. If you mail to a good target audience, the estimated return is 10 percent. For most, their money and effort are better spent elsewhere.

Should a group mailing still be something you want to pursue, instead of mailing out your postcard you may look into a packet marketing company. These companies will package a lot of ads together, and handle the stuffing of the envelopes, post-age (which they get cheaper by more easily qualifying for advertisement rates), and come up with a mailing list. These kinds of advertisements come in a business-size envelope that often has between ten and fifteen other slips of ad papers inside. If you price one of these services out and decide to go this route, be sure to budget for at least four mailings. Also be sure to offer a discount to people who bring in the coupon-like flyer they got in the mail.

Mining Future Customers from Current Customers

Anyone who attends your class is a potential future customer. Consider giving each attendee a short form to fill out that can help you guide that customer toward other classes. For example, if someone has enrolled in your puppy class, you need to know if they will, at a future date, have interest in agility or any other class you may teach. To gather this information, have the person state how many dogs in their household and the ages of the dogs. Then ask for information on events they'd like to learn about or other classes that they are considering taking. Always make sure during any class you teach that you have information available about other classes. But don't just overwhelm people with printed material that may or may not interest them. Instead find out what kinds of classes they may need or find out what their interest are. Then give them specific information, perhaps in the form of a well-crafted handout, that they can quickly read to determine if that class is indeed a good fit. Don't hesitate to follow up after you've given them information, just don't get pushy. Always be polite about a "no thank you."

Gift Certificates

One way to get your name out there as a dog trainer and obtain clients when you are just beginning a company is to give away your services. You can do that in the form of a gift certificate. But you are not simply going to randomly give away this gift of either a free class or a dog training consultation. What you will do instead is to trade that free gift certificate for a form of advertising. One way to do that is to donate a class or dog training session to a local dog fund-raiser. Many shelters or rescues looking to raise money will often hold a silent auction or some other kind of sales to raise funds. If you decide to do this, print up a professional-looking gift certificate to donate to the cause. Some computer software programs make that fairly easy.

Here are a few things you might want to make sure you do to make that gift certificate as effective as possible:

- Make sure all of your information is on that certificate. In fact, you might make it like a mini ad. For example, instead of briefly stating "good for one free class at Doggy Training Center" you can elaborate and list of the classes you offer.
- Give them a choice. Say something like "free for a class at Doggy Training Center," then list the classes they can choose from and briefly explain the advantage of that class. That way anyone looking over this gift certificate will know what classes you offer. Just be sure to keep your description brief. People are looking for information at a glance. Some ideas of what to state can include "Well-trained dogs don't just happen, but we can show you how to achieve a well-mannered dog using positive training techniques."
- Be sure to include your website on the certificate and your phone number. That way people who may not win the bid may decide to take down information.
- To better display this certificate, consider putting it in matting or an inexpensive frame so the charity can more easily display it. Also be sure to put on a six-month expiration date.

A Few Last Tips

Are you energized now about marketing? Before you decide to launch yourself into too many directions with your marketing efforts, below are a few basics that can help you with your planning:

- **Make a plan.** Make yourself a list of ideas for marketing your business. Perhaps some of the things I've mentioned above may strike you as something you'd like to use in your marketing endeavors. Or perhaps you have some of your own ideas. Once you compile that list, do a little research as to what each idea costs in both time and money. Now do some research into what is really going to work. While some of your competitors may not want to discuss ideas on marketing, similar businesses such as a groomer may take some time to talk to you to help you evaluate that list. As far as your competitors, look to see how they have marketed their businesses. Once you've done your list and your research, set up your budget. Remember, marketing isn't a one-time task, but an ongoing process.

- **Execute your marketing in stages.** The first stage may be to connect with vet offices. A few months later you may be at a dog event. At some time you may again reconnect with those vet offices. On an annual basis you may renew an ad in local dog magazines. So take some time to plot out your course of action, and keep with the task.

- **Know your audience.** Demographics have been mentioned from time to time. And again it bears mentioning: You need to understand your dog audience. What kind of training needs do they have and how can you fill those needs? As well, what are their expectations? Although you may be bargain minded, if your demographic wants the best at a fair price, then offering discounts will not entice them. Think about where your potential clients will most likely respond to your message. Will they look for this kind of information from a business card or a flyer? Will an ad in a local magazine catch their interest? Or do you need to reach them another way?

- **Don't base your marketing only on your opinion or your desires.** We are all aware that marketing companies exist that are hired by larger companies to get the message out. Although you are your own marketing company, don't limit yourself to advertising only in ways you feel your skills are best communicated. Diversify the kinds of marketing you do, and look toward others in the dog industry to find out what works for them.

- **Make sure you communicate how you are different from your competitors and the advantages of using your business.** Since you are not the only dog trainer in town, you need to find a way to set yourself apart from your competition. Look into what they say about themselves, or don't say about their classes, and make sure you communicate your strengths. For example, if you offer a puppy class, you may want to let the people know a bit about what the pup will learn. Tell them if you work on social skills, no-pull leash leading, and house-training troubleshooting. Think about what your clients need for their dog, and if you can fill that need, tell them about it.

- **Make sure you come across as credible.** Mention what makes you a competent dog trainer. Don't expect the people to only get that information from your bio page. If your customer is looking at your agility class, briefly state your accomplishments in agility so they know your abilities as an instructor.

- **Deliver a clear message.** Some of the components of delivering a clear message include saying something relevant, mentioning key issues more than once, and being consistent. To make sure your message is clear, have several people read it over and give you feedback. This is one time that just using a family member may have a downfall. Within close relationships there is already an understanding of unspoken meaning. To be sure that people outside your immediate relationships get your message, test it with someone you don't know, or don't know well. Perhaps a spouse's coworker will help, or

The Art of a Sale

At one time I worked with a man who had successfully worked for years in sales. Jim summed up his secret when he worked to capture a potential client's interest. He said, "When selling to people, sometimes you need to give them a certain amount of information so they know what they need from you. The key when using information to sell is to keep that information in a brief summary. Give your potential customer enough information so they realize that this is a viable opportunity. Just make sure you leave them with the feeling of needing a little more."

a sibling's friend will look things over. So look outside your immediate circle when you really need honest feedback about your marketing efforts.

There are a lot of options for marketing your business. It warrants taking some time to investigate what will work best for you. You will find that marketing demands investing both time and money. If you are just starting your business, have few clients, and lots of time, you might want to investigate things like Facebook and blogging. After all, they are free. As far as returns for this effort, you may find them like the mass mail, where you only get 10 percent or less clients brought in. If you already have clients, and are plenty busy, determine where best to spend your time for bringing in new clients based on your target audience. You might want to survey your current customers to see if they'd take time to keep in touch with you using either of these mediums. Be open and flexible with your marketing plan and be ready to explore new social media marketing opportunities as well as utilize the traditional methods to their fullest potential.

12

Behind the Scenes

From certifications to understanding what kinds of qualifications you need to hang out your shingle, a bit of behind-the-scenes information can help you navigate your career in dog training. But discovering what kind of an education you really need is only part of the equation. You need to learn how to evaluate educational opportunities to determine where to spend your time and efforts.

Qualifications for Teaching Classes

In the dog training business, you can call yourself a trainer and begin a class without any real qualifications or training. Of course, I'd not recommend you do that. Many dog trainers are self-taught. Even if you go to a school for dog training, it is up to you to ensure you have enough of the right kind of education. Before you decide what kinds of training can help strengthen you as a trainer able to teach a class, you first need to understand the class you plan on teaching. Some of the popular classes are described below.

Puppy Classes

These classes traditionally train both the people and the dog. Age limits for the dog typically mean your canine client will be anywhere from ten to fourteen weeks old. Most puppy classes require the dog to have begun their puppy vaccinations series. These young animals often come into the class an open book and the goal is to teach the dog the basics: sit down, stay, come when called, and how to accept a treat without biting. But the education of the dog owner is also part of the class. In this class you can get anywhere from first-time dog owners or dog owners who have had dogs before but not learned much about the correct ways to train, to dog owners who are fairly savvy or dog owners who may be trainers themselves but are looking for an opportunity to socialize a young dog. In general, you need to be prepared to train a majority of the humans as well as helping them to get their young dog's training started correctly. Included in your lessons should be house training, beginning the process of walking on a leash, and beginning socialization.

Skills and Knowledge You Need

You need to have some good, positive-based house-training techniques down. As well, you need to be able to train all of the basics using positive techniques. Puppies are dependent learners and naturally follow a good leader, making this is a good class to monopolize on that state of mind. You do not need a specialized certification for teaching this class. Most puppy classes are a good area for people to begin their training career. Both studies and on-the-job experience through mentoring help instructors learn their trade. The Sirius Puppy Training Redux video by Dr. Ian Dunbar has some good puppy class info.

Obedience

As mentioned before, when people say obedience they mean everything from the basic training of a dog to showing in competition. Although both disciplines teach a dog to sit and stay, there is a vast difference in the class goal and structure. Below you will learn about training puppies and progress to training for obedience classes for competition.

Intermediate Obedience Geared toward the Non-Competitor

This class can have several names, but is meant to be a follow-up to a puppy class. With very few exceptions, dog owners need both a puppy class and an intermediate class to get their pets trained correctly. Although the goals of puppy class are to teach the basics, the goal of the intermediate class is to get the dog through the canine teenage years or to reshape behavior in adults that have gone awry. Dogs in this class can vary from out of control to somewhat well behaved. The goal in this class is often to teach the dog good manners and self-control as well as round out good behaviors around other dogs. Some trainers offer more than one level for this class to help people train their more difficult dogs, sometimes breaking down classes into issues such as impulse control or walking well on a leash. Like the puppy class, this class typically deals with training the dog as well as teaching the dog owner good canine manners that include teaching a dog to greet other people and other dogs amiably.

As with the puppy class, a good way to learn is to be either an assistant, or to observe classes being taught in your area. By observing a lot of other people's classes, you can gather information as to what training you need to incorporate in your class, as well as get a feel for good ways to teach dog owners. As for your skills, you will often find you need to understand all the more in regard to how different breeds learn. Terriers, although often thought of as stubborn, really just have a different learning style that doesn't tolerate forcefulness as well as other breeds. Some breeds, such as your bully breeds, will need the right instruction at this stage to ensure the dog develops the right social interaction with other dogs. Dogs who are more socially challenged are typically not allowed in a regular intermediate class, but put into a specialized class to address the social issues such as excess aggression.

Competition Obedience Classes

Competition obedience classes teach both dog and owner how to compete at a dog show. There are several levels of obedience: sub novice, novice, open, and utility. Each level demands different tasks be preformed at a certain competency. Typically, teaching sub novice and novice classes is done in a regular weekly class. It isn't unusual for open and utility to be taught either weekly or as a drop-in class.

To teach competition obedience you need to show in these classes and ideally finish at the level you plan to teach. For example, if you want to teach novice obedience, you need to have a certificate earned after successfully scoring in three classes. With open and utility, there is more tolerance for people who are working at that level to also be teaching; however, ideally you would have earned at least one of your three legs.

Taking competition obedience classes is a good way to learn how to teach. Be choosy about your instructor. Find someone who others rave about and who has done well in competition. Some of these classes are taught by a judge who can often help you learn to put the right polish on the trained dog. Another way to learn more about obedience is to volunteer at shows as a ring steward. This allows you to discover the judge's perspective on the competition from several different judges, making your training class stand out from all others.

Agility

Agility classes teach both dog and owner how to compete at a dog show. Although there are different agility classes that include a diversity of equipment (UKC and AKC, for example, use some different equipment), similar things are typically stressed with agility training. In lower-level classes, introduction to the kinds of equipment is the goal. Following classes begin focus on the dog handler and dog working on that endless task of developing teamwork that makes the difference in a good run and faults in agility. No matter what kind of agility class the dog owner is working to compete in, from regular agility or a specialty like gamblers, dog handling skills always need to be honed.

The instructor is expected to have some kind of showing experience in agility. This is helpful in that experience gives the instructor a better understanding of the difficulty in mastering the skills needed, as well as how easy it is to miscue a dog. After that, what really makes a good agility instructor is a person's ability to read both people's body language and their dog's response. As well, this is a field where training the top agility dogs have experts in hot pursuit of the latest breakthrough in training techniques. The best agility instructors are continual students and often go to clinics to learn from people at the top of the field.

Skills and Knowledge You Need

You will need more than skills and knowledge to teach this class, you will need to have a lot of agility equipment. When acquiring your equipment find out what

What Is a Drop-In Class?

Drop-in classes serve a lot of people well and can help supplement your income as a trainer. Since some dog training, such as agility and the higher levels of obedience, require the dog handler constantly hone skills of both the dog and the handler, some people like a class they can come to when they have time, which allows them to practice their skills with their dog. Typically, it isn't unusual for the attendee to not commit ahead of time to the class, but instead pay a fee for each class attended. You, as an instructor, may need to have a class lesson in mind and, with obedience, may benefit by informing what parts of obedience practice you intend to highlight during a class. With agility, you will need to have courses in mind and may want to emphasize certain handling skills in each session. Drop-in classes can be good moneymakers for trainers, and often tend to have fairly consistent attendees.

the regulations are for different clubs. AKC, NADAC, UKC, and USDAA are the most common kinds of agility competitions offered, but check out your area. Learn what equipment is used at local shows. There can be differences in equipment height and small differences in design. Don't hesitate to query your class and make sure people are clear as to their goals to better prepare them for competition.

Where You Can Get Your Training

In addition to clinics, there are videos that break down training and training techniques. There are even specialized magazines to discuss agility, training, and training challenges.

Canine Good Citizen Classes

The Canine Good Citizen award is given through the American Kennel Club. To get this award people must have their dog perform at a certain level when tested on good manners and good reactions in several situations. Certification is often earned at different events offered in coordination with AKC. For most people, to attain success with this award they need to take the dog to a class that trains the dog in the correct way to respond in challenging situations. Simply working a dog toward this certification helps improve the dog's overall manners and behavior. A Canine Good Citizen certificate is generally required for dogs before they can be used as therapy dogs. Since this dog builds from obedience classes, to teach this class you first need to work with teaching general obedience and manners in dogs, and then be good at desensitization of dogs to various stimuli. Often, working as an assistant is a good way to learn for this class as well as studying desensitization techniques, including redirection. You should in the least attend a series of classes before trying to teach this class. Ideally you have a dog you have certified.

Independent Consulting

Perhaps you've seen the *Dog Whisperer* or *It's Me or the Dog*. Both programs show dog trainers going out to someone's home to solve canine issues that have made the family pet difficult or impossible to deal with. The people on these shows are doing independent consulting to solve dog behavior issues. People who do well in this field often have a diverse amount of experience in dog training before they go on to working with behavior problems. They also may need to rely on a bit of creativity as some of their canine clients can pose some unique challenges. When you do canine consulting you advertise yourself as a dog trainer or may even call yourself a canine behavior consultant. But calling yourself either a canine behavioral consultant or behaviorist should only be done if you actually qualify according to the industry guidelines. See page 149 for guidelines.

Independent consulting is not a business to undertake at the beginning of your dog career, but one that you may work into after you gain experience while teaching other dog classes. And although you may never get your own television show, you can create a reputation that puts you in demand for solving behavior issues.

To hone your skills in this area, be sure you have experience working with dogs at different behavioral stages and dealing with some of the developmental issues that can crop up. Take any courses in your area you can find. Go to clinics. Read books and watch videos. One helpful video is *Dog Aggression Biting* by Dr. Ian Dunbar. The APDT has a magazine that at times addresses problematic behaviors. Taking on project dogs or working with rescue groups or humane societies are other ways of getting started with hands-on experience.

Other Education Needed in Trainers

With so many breeds of dogs that can show up in a class, dog trainers need to be a pupil of several breeds and their basic natures. AKC has attempted to break down dogs in groups including working, terrier, toy, and sporting. You will find that a lot of dogs will fit into different learning categories, as well as find that there are different behaviors associated with what a breed of dog was originally bred to do. For example, herding dogs tend to have a higher chase drive, lending itself to more impulse-control issues. Guarding breeds, such as German shepherds, can have issues if dog owners don't do adequate socialization of the dog beginning when the dog is a puppy. Although many Labradors and golden retrievers often can behave well with little socialization compared to other breeds, some of the dogs that come from hunting lines may not behave the same as dogs bred for generations as pets. Any dog trainer worth his or her salt will find that learning about dogs is a lifelong pursuit and that studying insights discovered by other trainers can provide a fast track to a higher degree of expertise.

Places to Learn Your Skills

There are several places you can hone your skills. First off, be a reader. There are a lot of good books on dog behavior and dog behavior issues, from dogs who are too insecure to dogs who are aggressive. Find trainer-based magazines to help expand your education. Search for information online, but be aware that anyone can say anything unsubstantiated. If you decide to join a forum, find one that has several trainers who chime in.

You will benefit by going to dog training clinics. Explore all kinds of training from using electronic training collars to positive training. Study any good dog trainer you can and add them to your network.

Get ahold of training videos and learn everything from Tellington TTouch to clicker training. Dr. Ian Dunbar has a lot of literature about working with dog behavior issues as well as training. He hit the ground running with his more positive approach to training in an era where yank and spank was the norm. He also is responsible for the redirect technique that has a high value in dealing with unwanted aggression issues such as leash aggression. See chapter 10 for more information.

You will also benefit from going to conferences and lectures about specific topics, as well as seeking out magazines such as the one APDT puts out which shares other trainers' experiences. APDT holds an annual conference that covers a wealth of topics. Try to attend one. Volunteer to be an assistant at an area dog class that deals with aggression issues. The majority of the dog issues you will consult about deal with aggression. That isn't because there aren't a lot of other issues people need help with, but more because people too often don't call in help until they've experienced bites, vet bills, or dead dogs. Learn from dog catchers and their secrets to handling unwilling dogs. To do well in this field, you will find becoming well-networked is a great help. Having other dog trainers, in every discipline, can help you work through tough cases. To help round out your education, see if the humane society in your area (or some other dog shelter) offers classes in problem dog behaviors. Taking on rescues and foster dogs can also give you dogs to practice your skills on.

What Is a Behaviorist?

In the professional dog world, the term "behaviorist" is somewhat controversial. Some trainers call themselves behaviorists because they help clients modify their dog's behavior. Those behaviors can range from annoying, such as stealing food or jumping up, to more severe problems such as fear and aggression. Other trainers refrain from calling themselves behaviorists out of respect for "applied animal behaviorists" and "veterinary behaviorists"—two types of professionals who have met certain educational and certification requirements. One association that has worked to give the term behaviorist more specific meaning is the Animal Behavior Society (ABS). ABS requires a professional to possess a graduate-level education in ethology, learning theory, comparative psychology, psychology, biology, zoology, animal science, or experimental design, and to have a minimum of five years of professional experience before they call themselves a behaviorist. The ABS also has a program where behaviorists can become certified.

Certifications for Dog Trainers

There are a vast number of certifications for trainers in many disciplines. Different certifications can denote different levels of achievement. The listing below focuses on the more popular and readily accessible dog training. There are others, but these will give you a start. Be sure to check out the websites for more information.

- APDT (Association of Pet Dog Trainers) has certification for dog trainers called CPDT–KA Certified Professional Dog Trainer–Knowledge Assessed. For more information on Certified Professional Dog Trainer certifications, go to APDT.com.
- ABS (Animal Behavior Society) is the leading professional organization in North America for the study of animal behavior. There are two levels of certification: Associate Applied Animal Behaviorist and Certified Applied Animal Behaviorist. For more information, go to animalbehavior.org.
- CCPDT (Certification Council for Professional Dog Trainers) works to promote humane standards of competence for animal training and behavior professionals through criteria based on experience, standardized testing, skills, and continuing education, and identifies and markets those individuals to the public. The organization offers independent certification to animal training and behavior professionals. To seek certification from this organization, you must have a solid training history already in place, including hours of training experience as well as recommendations from three peers. Once certified, you are not set for life, but must re-certify every few years by way of demonstrating continued education in the profession. For more complete information on how to attain certification go to CCPDT.org.
- IAABC (International Association of Animal Behavior Consultants) has several certifications including CABC (Certified Animal Behavior Consultant), CDBC (Certified Dog Behavior Consultant), and CCAB (Certified Clinical Behavior Consultant) For more information, go to iaabc.org.

Organizations That Promote Specific Disciplines

NADOI (National Association of Dog Obedience Instructors), was founded in 1965 to promote modern, humane training methods and, at the same time, elevate the standards of the dog obedience instructing profession. Members of the organization require certain skills and knowledge of dog training and obedience instructing. NADOI offers certification for tracking, agility, and obedience certifications. At this time Rally is not offered. For more information, go to nadoi.org.

The Difference between a Real Dog Trainer and a Want-to-Be

Janice Dearth has quite a resume: AKC, ASCA, UKC Rally judge; all levels ASCA obedience judge; all levels AKC novice provisional obedience judge; all non-regular obedience classes; author of *The Rally Course Book, A Guide to AKC Rally Courses*; online Rally basics course instructor at e-trainingfordogs.com; and NADOI certified member 737 (where proof is in numbers of actual teams instructed, not just a written exam). She chimes in on what it really takes to be a dog trainer:

"You can take classes and you can take tests. The course work and pencil work can earn you a lot of letters behind your name in relatively short order. You can also attend the best of the best clinics and seminars, given by the best of the best in the dog training world, but that won't make you a dog trainer. A real dog trainer needs hands-on experience, lots of it. Working with many dogs, breeds, people, people and dogs. Different types of training goals. If your goal is training for Rally, then train a dog for Rally, compete in Rally with that dog, learn from it, train another or work with someone to train a dog for Rally, compete with it, and learn. Nothing is better than hands-on experience. Make sure you extend your experience to several breeds and to mixed breeds because different dogs will train differently and every dog you train has a lesson to teach you. Learn to work with hard-to-train dogs. Use positive training, food, toys, whatever motivates the dog. Each one is different. Not all dogs can be trained using these motivators. Then learn how to wean off the motivator for real life, or show ring, situations. You can't take food into the Rally ring or any show ring. A real dog trainer can teach a dog to work under all circumstances, eventually. Presence of a motivator cannot be a constant in real life. There are no shortcuts, only training."

Rally and Agility Organizations

At this time there are no organizations exclusively for Rally or Agility that have the same ranking as NADOI. Rally and Agility do have specifics you will need to train for different competitions. You need to get those specifics for agility from the different organizations that include NADAC (North American Dog Agility Council), UKC (United Kennel Club), AKC (American Kennel Club), and USDAA (United States Dog Agility Association). With Rally you need to go to organizations such as AKC and UKC to find out their specific requirements.

Dog Training Schools

There have been a variety of dog training schools that have cropped up in more recent years. Some are at universities, while other are taught by dog trainers who have designed their own courses. Some of these courses will help to get the neophyte dog trainer off to a good start while others will be inadequate for your educational needs. That being said, there is no one class that can substitute for the need to continually study dog training methods or the need to work hands-on with as many dogs as possible. However, to help you evaluate any courses you are considering taking, I asked Gail Fisher for some guidelines since she helped design and teach the first formal class at a university for dog training.

Gail will tell you that at in the late 1970s when she wanted to develop this class, she had to put a lot of effort into convincing the university to accredit the class. Her efforts back then truly helped pave the way for more classes to follow. Now it isn't unusual to find a variety of classes offered at different universities for training and working with canines.

In her All Dogs Academy, she now has three classes structured to benefit people when learning dog training: The first focuses on teaching dog training classes—teaching people how to train their dogs; the second course focuses on working with dogs—training a variety of different dogs; and the third focuses on behavioral consultation.

When it comes to attending a class that teaches you about training a dog, Gail explains that you need more than classroom instruction. You need lots of actual one-on-one, hands-on dog handling experience. Rather than learning how to apply your acquired education with one canine only, she recommends looking for a course that can offer you a variety of dogs to practice your new skills with.

Even if you go through all three of Gail's carefully designed classes and feel you have really excelled in your education, she has some additional educational advice: "Classes don't teach you to be a dog trainer, experience does—training dogs, lots of dogs. We tell our Academy students that it typically takes five years of experience training dogs to become a professional dog trainer. It takes years of practice with dogs, and dogs, and dogs. You need to work with different temperaments, ages, sizes, and breeds. This process never ends. No matter how many years we have been training, we still will find a dog with a different personality. What fun!" So even if you go to somewhere for a formal education, expect to keep working to get more hands on experience with a variety of dogs.

A Petsmart or Petco Education

Did you know that you can receive an education on how to be a dog trainer from Petsmart or Petco? Carol did just that and her story below can help you decide if this is an option for you.

Like many people, Carol found herself a victim of economic times. She held a good job in corporate America, but after a downturn in the economy, her well-paying corporate job disappeared. With little hope of regaining employment in her previous career, she decided to look for employment working with dogs. She had already done a lot of work through rescue organizations, and trained dogs for competitions such as obedience and agility. However, Carol knew since she had no other source of income other than her own employment, she couldn't spend the time so often necessary to build up a business to the point that it would pay her bills. So after a short time working at a large kennel, she decided to sign on with Petsmart.

Carol liked that the opportunity to pursue something she'd wanted to do all her life was now a means of survival. Petsmart provided Carol with affordable health insurance as well as other benefits, and covered the liability for her classes. She also didn't have to worry about less-busy times of the year, like the weeks before Christmas and during vacation times. Carol maintained a steady income because she also worked in the store during hours when she was not teaching.

As far as the training she got at Petsmart, Carol felt they offered a very good program on positive techniques. People who have little dog training experience can often successfully apply to the program. However, there is a downside. Trainers are commission and salaried. The salary is not very high, but there is a potential for income earning commissions per class sold. This gives the trainer incentive to sell in order to get commissions. Unfortunately, during down times of the year, Carol feels under the same pressure to make sales as the good times of year. Carol's job at Petsmart involves more than just dog training. She might be asked to help a customer buy a reptile, or run a register, or be able to help a customer select a bird food, or mop a floor.

If you are considering this option, ask yourself if you are the kind of person who enjoys the variety of responsibilities, or resents them. Also, be aware that you may be required to sign a "non-compete clause." This kind of clause may keep you from using your Petsmart or Petco training as a stepping stone for creating your own business. Carol didn't want to have her own business, so that issue was not a problem for her.

E-Training

Some people looking to become a dog trainer either can't find a nearby school where they can learn, or the classes that are offered are not high quality. There are several sites that are now offering dog training classes online to fill trainers' needs. But can you really learn efficiently in this manner? And if you want to take an online class, which ones are worth the money? I wondered this myself. To find answers, I called up the owner of e-trainingfordogs.com. After talking with Dr. Cheryl Asmus Aguiar, I came away with a few ideas about what to look for if you are considering online training.

Cheryl comes from a strong academic background with a lot of teaching experience in both dog training and human training. Cheryl has designed her classes using expert instructors. Some classes are offered as a live class. In that class setting the student listens to and speaks with the instructor online in a virtual classroom where there are other students. A PowerPoint presentation and video clips are given in real time while listening to the instructor either via a telephone conference call or through VOIP (Voice Over Internet Protocol). You will be able to ask questions and receive answers in real time. Live classes meet at set days and times. Assignments, quizzes, and examinations are completed at set intervals.

She also offers on-demand classes that are recorded classes. With these classes, you can't listen to the class or be able to speak with your instructor in real time. Instead, you watch the class at a time convenient for you. Assignments are completed at your pace, and there are quizzes and examinations. Videos are e-mailed to an instructor who can give you feedback on course exercises.

What I liked about this online dog training site is that Cheryl has brought a lot of educational expertise to it. I feel she has worked to make sure the courses she offers are top quality. I also like the idea that she works to give a student the opportunity to get instructor feedback. Without feedback or some kind of interaction, I see no advantage to taking an online course over reading a book or buying a video.

However, I wanted to get more of a feel for how well e-learning could work. So I asked someone who had taken Rally classes the usual way to try out the Rally class offered at www.e-trainingfordogs.com. Below is that person's critique.

I (name withheld) was asked to compare the online Rally-O through www.e-trainingfordogs.com course to a traditional Rally class I took a year ago. The traditional class had one instructor for a group of ten dog/handler teams. I have experience with other online courses taken through an accredited university via an online degree program.

Taking the online Rally-O course was a lot of fun and I would recommend it for busy people. E-trainingfordogs.com offered three different ways to take the course. The least expensive was Audit OnDemand with 30 days access to OnDemand course. With this class, no homework was required nor was there feedback from the instructor. The second, more expensive class was an Audit OnDemand. This class had three-months access to the OnDemand course. No homework required or feedback from instructor was offered. The class I took was the most expensive. This class was For Credit OnDemand and offered six-months access to OnDemand course. Homework was required which assessed your knowledge and skills. The class included one-on-one feedback from the instructor. I know from my online degree program that requiring homework and providing feedback helps motivate people to do the work and do it well. It is hard for people to perform the best and take all the material if there is no test/graded feedback.

The online Rally course had eight fifteen-minute courses that you watched, then took a short quiz. The instructor included short videos demonstrating the specific components of the lesson for that class. Additional documents for reading were also available. Once you passed a quiz, you could access the next course. Below are my comparisons for the traditional class and the online class.

Comparisons

- *When taking a class in person, you get immediate feedback from the instructor. The advantage of recording your lesson is that the instructor has full attention of what you are doing and you won't miss something if the instructor is working with someone else. Feedback from the online course took less than a week to receive.*

- *A regular class gives you the opportunity to train in a highly distracting environment. This may or may not be a good idea. When you are initially training a task, distractions are not a good thing. For initial training, the online class, which takes place in a control situation such as your house, has an advantage. However, with a dog that has the basics down, a class situation allows the dog to learn how to follow commands in the presence of other dogs, much like the dog would experience in competition. Perhaps an ideal situation is to do the initial training with the online material, then move on to a traditional class.*

- *Having a "bad night" can easily impact the overall training relationship with your dog. Some dogs are very sensitive and can take several steps back from one bad training experience, which might occur if your class happens to fall on a night when you have no business trying to train a dog. Since regular classes are on a schedule, you can't as easily skip out on those bad nights. With the online class you are on your own schedule. This allows you to do training at more ideal times. Additionally, if your dog decides to regress in training, you can remain at that lesson level rather than having to move on with the rest of the class.*

- *In the regular class I took, I disagreed with the instructor's use of choke chains and jerking on leash to get sits from a stubborn dog with motivation issues (yes, my dog is one of those more stubborn breeds). With the online class, there was no one standing over me to argue on this issue. Since I am a more experienced trainer, I found the online training let me use techniques that I knew worked the best on my dog. That being said, some instructors do bring good techniques to a regular class, and if you have a good instructor, you may benefit from specific real-time guidance with your dog.*

- *Online classes can have an advantage for people who get very nervous in front of other people or for any other reason feel self-conscious in a regular dog training class. When I am first training a new dog, my stress can have a disadvantage. However, if I have practiced at home, then tackle the stress of being in front of people, I find I can better control my nervous energy, especially once I've honed my skills with my dog. This can make doing the e-training an advantage over a regular class.*

- *Both kinds of classes had a review at the beginning of the lesson, but only the online class outlined what was going to be taught for this class. An outline of the lesson you are about to learn is a good technique.*
- *Both kinds of classes taught similar material and demoed both the Rally signs and training methods. The online was more consistent about the training method demos. Both in a regular class and online, some of the demo dogs were not perfect, resulting in faults in the demo. The advantage of the online course was that the instructor continued to perform the activity until the right behavior was achieved (no discipline just retry and sometimes with additional cues), then gave the dog the right level of award (a verbal "good job" and sometimes jackpot).*

Online Course Comments

- *The instructor knew the material and understood how to teach, was prepared, and had an enthusiastic attitude without being chirpy. You felt like the instructor valued both your time and the instructor's time, and kept a very professional manner. There was no condescension in the approach.*
- *The course material was taught at an efficient pace.*
- *The instructor had demonstration videos, simple PowerPoint slides, and good flow when talking (didn't speed up or slow down, stutter, or have long pauses between).*
- *The lessons themselves were short, between fifteen minutes and thirty minutes. Practice time added to the lesson, but could be done at my pace. If I felt I'd gotten saturated by new information, I could quit when I wanted or if my dog needed.*
- *The online class ensured all the rules were clear, with specific explanations of how rules can apply to each of the new obstacles being taught. This was valuable as there was more weight on rules/judging, what can get you NQ, and what judges are looking for.*

- *Additionally, each Rally sign taught was demonstrated at least once. It was easy to see that the instructor was familiar with various size dogs and how different dogs accepted training as well as different dog demeanors. I liked the training tips.*

Aspects Needing Improvement

- *It was difficult to get the video recording of my class assignments to the course instructor. Videos are large sizes and the method used was difficult to use, or had to be retried.*
- *After you submitted a lesson, you didn't get any confirmation that lesson was received. Once the lesson got to the instructor, it took too long to get feedback. It is important to get grading/feedback on assignments before the next one is assigned or due.*
- *This course assumed a working relationship, knowledge of Rally, etc. It would have been helpful if the expected abilities of the student were made very clear prior to taking the class.*
- *I feel they could have offered a more interactive feedback process such as Skype or even FaceTime, especially if there are reoccurring problems in a performance. That kind of immediate feedback would allow me to keep trying till I got it right.*

As a dog trainer, you are your business. Your level of education will help you conduct a business people will seek out. As your education and expertise grow with your dog skills, you will find opportunity to grow your business. The next chapter can help you with learning what you need to do when growing your business.

13 Growing Your Business

Perhaps when you decided to take on the challenge of your own dog training business, you looked at someone else's already established business and envisioned yourself in their shoes. What you saw in their business was a vision that had materialized over time. For most people taking on a business for the first time, or launching into a new business, starting small can make the difference between success and failure. With your home-based dog training business, as you find opportunities to grow, be sure to do a little planning to keep that growth at a healthy pace as well as reach your long-term goals. Fortunately, beginning a dog training business as a home-based business is the ideal way to travel the road to success. It is, of course, a good idea to set out with a good roadmap for your journey.

The Advantage of Starting Small

When you are new to being a business owner, there are several advantages to starting small. There is a lot of learning and there are growing pains. Even if you've had a different kind of small business before, you'll find the dog training business has its own unique demands. If this is your first business endeavor, you'll find that being a business owner will teach you things about yourself. Beginning your smaller, home-based business offers opportunities to learn without suffering mistakes that can cost you financially. By traveling at a steady pace, you may find opportunities you hadn't envisioned at first that can add to your bottom line. Likewise, you may eliminate some of the business directions you thought might work out, but no longer fit the business you've grown into.

Selling Equipment

Dog training is a service business where you are selling your service to a customer. But there is also an opportunity to sell more. Training classes often need equipment. If people show up to the class and don't have the right equipment, the effectiveness of that class can be greatly compromised. Since a lot of classes are part of a lesson plan, and that lesson won't be repeated, value can be lost if the right equipment isn't available. So don't hesitate to offer to sell equipment to your clients, especially when it helps your bottom line.

I've seen how sales can benefit both trainers and customers first-hand. Many people come to an intermediate class with out-of-control dogs. Often the use of a head halter can help them get their dog back under control. When used correctly, some head halters can even help back down aggressiveness. Ironically, I found myself making head halter sales in my puppy class, where I didn't expect to need that device. Two sales I clearly remember were to people who had physical challenges. One person had severe arthritis and couldn't take any pulling or tugging on a leash by her rambunctious golden retriever. The other sale was to an older couple who couldn't use lure training to get their terrier to follow alongside. Part of their problem was they couldn't bend over. Using a head halter made it possible for them to walk the dog in the park. Other sales were made to participants who, although they attended the classes, wouldn't take the time needed to train their dog outside of the class. Rather than have them stop walking their dog because the puppy pulled excessively, I sold them a head halter. By stocking these devices for sale, you can let the dog owner try the device before buying to see how that device can work for them. I like to stock both Gentle Leader collars and Halti harnesses. I've had some people buy both.

I've already discussed selling agility equipment. What you may want to do with these kinds of more expensive equipment is to list prices and show pictures on a bulletin board. That way the customer knows that you sell them without you having to sound too much like a salesperson. Keep in mind that it is best to try and sell the same equipment the student is currently using. And don't forget near the end of the class to ask if people are interested in bundling an order to save on shipping. Be sure to get your money in advance on any order and to explain that there is no refund once the order is placed should they change their mind. That is just good business. If they feel they no longer want the item, you can offer to let them sell it by posting it on your bulletin board, and you may even offer to let them leave it at your facility and handle the resale transaction yourself. However, once they order an item, it becomes their item. Just make that clear on your order forms so there are no hard feelings.

Offering Other Dog Services

After you get your business established, you may find clients asking for other training opportunities. If these opportunities are ones you wouldn't mind teaching, then stay ahead of the game and work toward educating yourself in areas where you can expand your business. In short, let your business lead you where your heart wants to go, and don't be surprised if you discover areas to work with dogs you didn't think of when first designing your business.

If you want to expand your business, but don't know which way to go, then do a little research to get a sense of needs in the dog community. For example, a lot of people are pulled around by their dogs, especially when they take them to the veterinarian. You may work to team up with a few vets and design a class that teaches dogs to have manners with their vet visits. Such a class would probably include working with dogs who pull on a leash and teaching dogs to stand on the weighing scale. You can also teach people how to get their dog used to having their paws and mouth being handled to make nail trimming and teeth brushing easier. If you can get the vet community behind these kinds of training classes you will have better luck filling your classes.

Another opportunity that often arises when you teach classes is to do private lessons. Those can vary from doing simple behavior training with an unruly dog to doing work with more severe problems. People who teach classes often find themselves approached by their current clients. Perhaps the client has issues because of a multiple-dog household and has seen some squabbles now that the one dog taking classes has reached adolescence. There are a number of reasons that teaching classes opens opportunities for private consultations. You need to determine if you want to do this kind of work, then set your rates ahead of time so you are not caught off guard if someone asks for this service. It comes across a lot more professionally if you don't talk as if this has never occurred to you, as opposed to someone ready to discuss what you can and can't do.

Adding Staff

You may already have helpers in your class who are not paid. Perhaps you found that help from a family member, or an apprentice, or a volunteer. As your business grows, you will come to a point when you need to hire help. Adding staff can offer you a chance to grow your business beyond your teaching abilities. If you go about it correctly and if you learn how to hire the right people, staff can help your business run smoothly.

Know the Right Interview Questions

Interviewing is both an art and a science. Large companies hire agencies to give seminars on how best to interview, and books on the subject are pricy. Learning some of the finer aspects of interviewing can help you find the right employee. Begin your search for that ideal employee by first getting a clear idea of the qualities and skills you need from your employee. That will help you know the right questions to ask to help you secure a good employee.

The Art of Interviewing

Interviews are conducted to help decide if someone is the right fit for the position you need to fill. Although "yes" and "no" questions are one way of obtaining information, the skilled interviewer learns how to ask what is known as "open-ended questions." These questions literally open the door for your potential candidate to share parts of themselves that yes and no questions don't reveal.

Open-ended question start with what, how, when, why, and where. These invite the person you are interviewing to disclose more about themselves than a simple yes or no. For example, rather than ask "Are you willing to work weekends?" Ask instead, "Under what circumstances are you not able to work weekends?" The first question may be answered by your candidate with an honest "yes" because the person you are interviewing may not be looking at things that come up and cause problems. The second question may reveal an answer such as, "The one weekend a year I really can't work into my schedule is the weekend I travel to the national Boston Terrier show." This will allow you to decide if you can work around exceptions rather than find out later that some of the exceptions are going to become a hardship on your business.

Other type questions you may want to ask are accomplishment questions. For example, instead of asking a potential trainer, "Have you dealt with problematic dog owners in a training class before?" To which you will probably get a yes. Ask the question more open-endedly. Ask, "Can you give me an example of a situation where you had to deal with a problematic dog owner in a training class and how you handled the problem?" The answer to the open-ended style of question will give you a lot more information about how this person will or will not work out in your business.

As you put together your questions for future employees, be sure to ask your potential employee what their long-term goals are. You need to be sure that their future plans are going to work out well with your needs. If the person states they plan on only working in this position for six months to a year, that may impact your decision to take them on, or at least give you a heads-up that if you do take them on for the short term, you'll need to continue your search for a more permanent employee.

What You Need in a Dog Assistant

Before you begin your search for a dog assistant, you need to sit down and do a bit of analysis as to exactly what you want. Take a few minutes to jot down what kind of things your new employee needs to be able to do, and what kinds of skills they need to have. This will help you in your search for a good fit for your business, and help you ask the right kinds of questions. Be sure to make a list of the duties you require for the job. Some potential employees may have one concept about what they will be doing and if you have another, this can leave you hiring someone who just doesn't work out. Hiring and then letting go of an employee is a very time-consuming process that doesn't bring in any additional revenues. In fact, hiring the wrong employee is such a big issue that large companies spend a lot of money educating their supervisors on how to better select the right person for the job. Some of the things to ask yourself when looking for an employee:

- Do I want someone who will stay at this level or do I want someone who may work into a different position in the future?
- Will this person's schedule work with my needs? Often classes are held in the evening and weekends and assistants need to understand they may have to work most weekends.
- Do I want someone who contributes his or her ideas to my class or only follows mine?
- Can this person meet any physical demands of the job?
- Do I need someone who may have additional talents that can help with my business?

When looking to find an assistant, draw on your dog community. Work with people in your network. Advertise in area dog newsletters. Also, consider contacting your local dog 4-H clubs. See if there is someone who is near graduation from high school or has recently graduated from high school that the 4-H leader can recommend as a good dog handler.

How to Train or Acquire Another Trainer

One of the best ways to secure a trainer who closely follows your own preferred training philosophies is to acquire that person as an assistant then groom them for the job. Other places to find dog trainers are at shows. Everyone from judges to ring volunteers may have the desire and skills to do dog training. At shows you can often observe how these people interact with their own dogs. You may also want to network with your dog community. Send out the word you are looking to hire a trainer. As with your dog assistant, you may want to put an ad in local dog club newsletters.

Non-Competitive Clauses

A non-competitive clause or covenant is an agreement between an employee and employer not to compete. Typically this kind of an agreement is one which some employers ask employees to sign as part of the terms of employment. The use of such clauses is premised on the possibility that upon their termination or resignation, an employee might begin working for a competitor or start a business that will compete with yours. Since they have access to your clients and your techniques, this can give them a competitive advantage if they choose to abuse confidential information about their former employer's operations or sensitive information such as customer/client lists, business practices, upcoming products, or marketing plans.

A non-competitive clause is used to help protect your business. For example, if you take on a dog trainer who becomes popular with his or her teaching methods, and that dog trainer at some point decides to take off and form his or her own business, you may find that most of the participants in that class have just left. You, as the business owner, have just lost revenue. You spent time and money building up that original clientele. You may have helped hone the trainer's skills to the point they are now. You did marketing to get that class off and running and now all that time and money has left with your now ex-trainer. Making matter's worse, you need to again recruit a new trainer. Those are some of the reasons that businesses have their workers sign a non-competitive clause.

If you decide to do a non-competitive clause, make it fair to both parties involved. Too restrictive of a clause may keep you from hiring some of the better trainers. Some things to include may be that the trainer can't take any current clients with him or her for a period of six months. Other competitive clauses work to restrict geographic locations. Imagine your former trainer setting up shop next door. However, you need to make the distance reasonable, such as twenty-five miles. Keep in mind that the extent to which non-competitive clauses are legally allowed varies per jurisdiction. If you are considering a non-competitive clause, you will be well served to consult a lawyer.

Hiring Employees Means Paperwork

Hiring employees requires you have them fill out a couple of forms. The Immigration Reform and Control Act 1986 (IRCA) required employers to verify that all newly hired employees present "facially valid" documentation verifying both the employee's identity and the employee's legal authorization to accept employment in the United States. That is done is by using an I-9 form, the Employment Eligibility Verification Form. You can download this form at www.uscis.gov/files/form/i-9.pdf. Be aware that this paperwork needs to be done at the time you hire the employee, so don't put it off. In addition, you must complete Section 2 within three days of starting work. As an employer you are responsible for ensuring that the forms are completed properly, and in a timely manner. Two forms of identification are required with the forms and you need to keep those in the employee's file. Typically a pictured drivers license, a copy of a birth certificate, and a Social Security card all work as acceptable identification. The I-9 is not required for unpaid volunteers or for contractors.

The other form you need your employees to fill out is called a W-4. This form can be downloaded at www.irs.gov/pub/irs-pdf/fw2.pdf. The W-4 document tells you how much income tax an employee wants withheld from their paycheck. It often works well to keep both the I-9, the employee's identification, and the W-4 in an employee file. Keep these records even after the employee no longer works for you.

Paying Employees

Hourly and salary designations as well as subcontract and independent contract employees all have rules as to how you pay that employee. Understanding those rules may help you decide which kind of employee will work best in your business.

Hourly Employees

When you pay an employee by the hour, you are required to withhold income taxes, pay unemployment tax, and match the Social Security and Medicaid tax that you withhold. You also need to pay workman's compensation insurance should the employee become injured on the job. This certainly seems like a lot of extras above and beyond the hourly wage, and indeed it is. That is one of the reasons an hourly wage is so much less than what you would pay an independent contractor or a subcontractor.

People who hate bookwork tend to hate figuring payroll and dealing with employee withholding all the more. However, if you find doing your own accounting manageable, you will find that doing payroll is something you can also learn. Even if you decide to hire out this task, you need to make sure you understand the basics enough to ensure the job is done correctly and reports are filed on time.

If you have never done payroll, consider asking for help. Certainly you can obtain all of the forms you need for filing online, but you may find it a lot easier to do if you have someone help you through the process the first time. Some resources you may consider include having an accountant or bookkeeper assist you on learning how to do payroll correctly. There are also software programs that do payroll calculations making your job easier. There are even online payroll services. However, for most small business, the online services charge too high of a minimum fee to make them practical.

Can You Hire an Hourly Employee and Still Avoid Payroll?

There is another option to taking on a regular employee without taking on the obligation of employee taxes. You can do this by hiring the employee through a temporary employment agency. You begin by contacting the temp agency, and telling them you want to hire a specific person through them. The temp agency does all the employee paperwork and pays all the payroll taxes. You pay the agency an hourly fee for the employee which reflects their costs and the hourly wage the employee receives. Although fees vary, you will oftentimes pay something in the neighborhood of $16–17 an hour for an employee who receives $10 an hour. For some people, not having to deal with the employment taxes, employee forms, and sending out W-2s at the end of the year is worth the money spent. Temp agencies even handle background checks and references as well as help with the interviewing process. However, be aware that some agencies have liability issues if the employee works in your home. This is certainly something to check into if you rent a training facility. Another advantage is that if the person doesn't work out after all, you simply tell the temp agency you want to let that person go.

Hiring a Subcontractor or Independent Contractor

You must withhold taxes for employees, but if you hire a subcontractor or independent contractor, you do not withhold taxes. This can create a tempting relationship to form with your employees. Simply calling them either an independent contractor or a subcontractor, write them a check for gross pay, and you are done. But, business owners can get themselves into problems if they try to label what the government sees as a regular employee as either an independent contractor or a subcontractor. Knowing the rules can keep you out of IRS and other legal hassles.

Independent contractors are self-employed. A good example of that kind of worker would be if you hired people to come and clean your facility on a monthly basis. These people most likely do this for other people in a similar capacity. You expect them to show up with all their own equipment and leave the place clean. Although you may make requests for certain areas where you want specific attention for cleaning or that they use dog-friendly cleaning solutions, for the most part, they know how to do the job without you saying anything. If you decide to hire an independent contractor for your dog business, that person should be someone who offers a class that you want at your facility, but you don't manage them the way you would a regular employee. You will not tell the instructor how to do his or her job. True independent contractors will often design their own class. To best decide the guidelines for this kind of a relationship, you are wise to consult a lawyer.

Subcontractors

More often, dog training businesses look to hire subcontractors for their business. Again, you need to exercise caution and may want to consult a lawyer to make sure you are meeting all of the requirements for calling someone a subcontractor. In general, a subcontractor performs the work of the principal contractor under the control of the principal as to the details of the work performed. If you hire a subcontractor, you can design the class to be taught, and then let the subcontractor carry out the teaching of the class. This person, while performing the duties of a subcontractor, will not be under your direct supervision.

Since a subcontractor isn't an employee, you are wise to construct an agreement between you and the subcontractor. Elements in that agreement may include the type of class taught, the time structure for teaching the class, payment arrangement such as total pay at the end of the class, or halfway through and then the balance at the end. With your regular employees, if they can't make a class, it is your responsibility to find or approve a substitute, or to make sure the class is rescheduled. With a subcontractor, you can expect them to carry out that duty and need to make that clear in your contract. You may include fines for breach of contract, and you may have behavioral guidelines. This contract needs to be signed for each class undertaken. You can expect a subcontractor and a contractor to carry their own liability insurance and need to keep a copy on file.

An Important Note about Insurance

Both subcontractors and independent contractors need to also have their own workman's compensation policies. If you hire someone who is supposed to be an independent or subcontractor, but don't make sure they have their own workman's compensation policy, then you risk that this person will be viewed by the government as an employee instead of a contractor. When looking to have a subcontractor or independent contractor, you may be wise to have both your accountant and your lawyer make sure all legalities are in order. Failure to clearly establish a correct relationship between a contractor or an independent contractor can make you, as the business owner, liable for unpaid payroll taxes should the government deem this relationship is actually an employee-employer relationship.

Health Insurance and Benefits

In 2010, President Obama signed new regulations for health care reform. These regulations affect small business requirements for carrying health care for employees. Some of the changes will not go into effect until 2014. To make sure you are complying with current laws, visit sba.gov.

If you only need to provide health care insurance for yourself, and/or your family, keep in mind the larger the group covered by health care insurance, typically the more affordable the insurance becomes. To look for affordable insurance, check out any organizations you belong to, especially national organizations to see if they offer group health policies. You may also contact an independent insurance agent who specializes in health insurance to see if he or she can find a way to combine your coverage needs with a larger group to help bring down costs.

The Family Factor with Small Business Employees

People who work at large companies often form relationships with coworkers. Small businesses also create relationships between employees, but those relationships more often mirror that of an extended family. Just as you as a small business owner need to wear many hats, your employees are often called upon to do a diversity of different tasks, often beyond their original job description. The willingness of an employee to do this can make or break a smaller business.

Because you will often need to ask more of your employees, just as you probably have with your family when soliciting their help, you will find that your extended family-like relationship will work in your favor. Since you will be asking employees to give extra, in return, you need to treat them with a higher regard than a large company with the attitude that anyone can easily be replaced. From kennel help to your highest-paid trainer, work to let them know they are all an important part of your business.

Motivating Your Employees to Do Their Best

The discussion about the family factor in a small business touches upon the concept of needing to motivate your employees to do their best. Ironically, motivating your employees has a lot of commonalities with motivating dogs. Some employees, like some dogs, are somewhat self-motivated to do certain things because they find those tasks self-rewarding. For example, if you have an employee who teaches one of your classes, and that employee loves teaching that kind of class, then the task is self-rewarding. That doesn't mean that the employee doesn't need encouragement to seek your help should they have issues with people attending the class. Since some instructors are at a level where they more readily take charge, you may need to encourage them to come to you with certain issues rather than going it alone.

As a dog trainer, I hope you can see that when working with a dog, the best approach is to teach the action you want as opposed to reprimanding the behaviors you don't want. The same is true with your employees. Tell them what you want, rather than assume they can read your mind. When they comply, give rewards. Though this may sound tongue-in-cheek in that the process so closely mirrors positive-training techniques, I'm am not trying for humor. A positive approach to working with your employees goes much further in motivation than a negative approach. Also, just like with dog training, should that employee do something you don't like, don't reprimand them. Instead, give them your feedback in a positive way.

Holding a Staff Meeting

One way to help keep the harmony of your employees intact is to hold staff meetings. A staff meeting allows people to become better organized and make sure that all the tasks are delegated to different people. By talking things over at a staff meeting, you can invite feedback from individuals, and have the opportunity for all of the employees to offer input. Since in very small businesses all employees are important, you can let them know that their input in the meeting is highly valued.

Staff meetings are a great way to touch bases with everyone as a group. This is a good time to invite people to bring up issues that the group may need to resolve. But don't let this become personalized. This is not the time for one person to complain about another's activities. Make it clear to your staff that those kinds of issues need to be addressed with you more privately. Staff meetings are more about how to keep the business running as efficiently as possible.

A couple of do's and don'ts. Do take time to praise activities that are working well for a business. Don't praise only one person, instead find a way to spread out the acknowledgment of all your employees' contributing efforts. Don't ever bring up issues that should be handled one-on-one. This is never a time to criticize or

Correcting Employee Problems

Just as certainly as you need to show good leadership when working a dog, you need to show good leadership with your employees. Some of that leadership may mean working to correct an issue with a particular employee. Letting problematic actions by any one employee go without correction is not only counterproductive to your business, it can cause discontentment with other employees. When approaching an employee about a problem, keep a few things in mind: Don't make this a me-versus-you event; be polite. Tell them the issue at hand and talk about ways to change to correct the issue; don't put them on the defensive when talking about the issue; use terminology such as "there is a problem that has come up" rather than "you are creating a problem"; make sure you listen to what they have to say about the issue instead of approaching the issue already assessing their guilt and having decided on a form of punishment or a reprimand. It is better to solicit cooperation than to leave an employee feeling alienated over an issue.

reprimand. If something needs to be changed, invite ideas, instead of complaining about what you don't like. Do make sure you bring some kind of refreshments if the meeting lasts more than half an hour. After all, who doesn't like a cookie?

Concluding Thoughts

If you picked up this book as the first step to pursuing your dream as a dog trainer, I hope you have found more than you expected and now feel better educated about how to succeed in your business. Great efforts were taken in this book to include all the aspects of conducting a successful business in dog training. If you already have a dog training business but are not happy with how your business is growing, I hope you have found information to get you back on track. After reading the contents up to the end of this chapter, you will find yourself filled with a lot of information and perhaps have new perspectives and ideas as to where you can take a dog training business. In appendix A you will find roundtable questions I asked three other dog trainers who are at different stages of their journeys. One person is balancing her job as a mother with her desires for a career in dog training. Another is someone close to the end of her journey. And a third tells how she transitioned from a more traditional job into a successful dog training business. If you ever doubted that you can fulfill your personal journey, you need to take a look at all three of these women's stories. One of them has had stellar success. All three interviews address different aspects of the information in this book, and each can help you better understand where you may be able to take your dreams.

Appendix A:
Roundtable Questions

Up to this point in the book, you've been introduced to a lot of information about ways to start your home-based business, much of which reflects my own personal experiences. As you embark upon your own endeavor, you probably wished you had a crystal ball so you could look ahead and see how different choices you make might play out. After all, armed with some of the information in this book, you still have a lot of choices as to how you will conduct your business. To help you make some of those choices and to help you envision your future, I've interviewed three people who have traveled parts of the path you are looking to undertake with their home-based dog training businesses. Their original stories are in chapter 1. Below are the answers to specific questions about their business.

Michelle Douglas, Owner of Refined Canine

Do you do your own bookkeeping?

"Yes, I do. Always. But not my own taxes. I use an accountant for that."

What fueled your decisions?

"The cost factor."

Have you always done the bookkeeping this way?

"Yes."

What is the background that helped you? Did you use an accountant to help you?

"I didn't use an accountant to help me. I took a course at the university."

Is your business where you expected it?

"Not exactly. When I first started out I hoped to be a lot further along on my path to financial independence. But, when I decided to have children, my goal shifted. From the time I decided to start a family, I no longer expected to go along as quickly as I initially planned. My primary goal is to raise my children and be there for them. Although training is my primary job, and it is a full-time job, it is still a part-time endeavor."

How many years have you been in the dog training business?

"Fifteen years on my own, plus one year as a student."

What are your future plans?

"Now that my youngest is three, and going to preschool part time, I hope to use my extra time to work on growing my business again. Most of my business comes from referrals right now. This year, I plan to re-establish my relationships with some of the local vets. I plan on shifting my focus to private lessons. As I make more money, that will allow me to reinvest in the business."

Michelle added, "I accept the fact that hobbies, free time and work all need to be the same thing. I realize that I don't have the time to run a successful, or semi-successful business, raise a family, and pursue outside interests. While my husband has free time to play in a band and ride his motorcycle, my free time is when I run my classes and do my private lessons, which is work, but I enjoy it. But you have to enjoy it otherwise you will burn out."

When you began your business (or at any time), did you do a business plan? If not why?

"I started to. I actually went to the small business resource center in my area and met with someone. That person gave me a small booklet on how to write a business plan. I began the process, but never formally put it into a written plan. Toward the end of last year I began working with a business coach to get something more formalized. Rather than a business plan, he did a 'blueprint' for me to illustrate my priorities and weaknesses. Right now, he has me working on 'billable hours' and time management, as well as getting myself into vets' offices to get face-to-face with office staff."

Did the work you did on your business plan help you?

"I think it did. That work gave me more of an all-encompassing perspective of all the different factors I needed to think about. It isn't just putting an ad in the paper and teaching classes, which may work for some. I realized that when growing a business, there was a lot more I had to think about, that I hadn't thought about up to that point."

What were the biggest surprises with starting your business?
"I think that realizing that there were many more steps involved than I thought. Even just renting a building. You don't just pay the rent. There are a lot more costs like electricity and hot water. After trying to rent a space for training, with the rental so high, I found I needed to charge too much for many classes. I found out what worked better for me was to work through the local recreation center."

What were the biggest challenges with starting your business?
"Budgeting. That is still a bit of a challenge for me."

Are you a sole proprietorship, LLC, partnership, or corporation? Has this status changed over the course of your business?
"I started as sole proprietorship then became an LLC. That was easier than I thought. I saw an advantage of having a separation between me and my business."

Were there any unique customers or category of customer issues you'd like to share an experience about?
"When I first started I learned my techniques from a traditional training school where we used choke collars and made leash corrections. I realized that my dog would do everything I told her to do, but she was clearly not enjoying what we were doing. I went to my first APDT conference and I did a one-eighty. I changed my techniques, completely eliminated metal collars, and took a more 'purely positive' attitude and philosophy into my instruction. But, in the last couple of years I've had a couple of clients, one in particular, who taught me that I didn't always know what was best."

Michelle added, "One client, a woman, had a ninety-plus pound pit bull that was chewing up the cabinetry. So I did a work up for an entire behavior plan. When I went into her house I saw her prong collar hanging on the wall. I told her the first thing we needed to do was to change away from that. I told her that her relationship with her dog was going to be harmed every time she took her dog for a walk down the street. But that was my prejudice at that point. We did three lessons of trying to desensitize her dog to wearing a body harness or head halter. But this dog found these things unbelievably aversive. The entire time his body would get so uncomfortable. This was breaking the communication the dog and owner did have when I met them. So I said, 'You know what? Go get your prong collar and put it on him. I just want to watch him walk down the street.' I wished I'd videotaped it. Because positive trainers do not believe me when I say that this dog was so happy. He was wiggly. He was looking at her and expressed (with this body language), 'Yeah, we are going to go for our walk. It's our walky collar.' She didn't need to correct him. He never even pulled tight on that collar. Just putting it on him, he watched her and she was able to walk with that dog. She could have held the leash with one finger. She said to me, 'Yeah, this is the way we used to walk until you told me to stop trying to use this collar. I certainly didn't want my dog to have a negative association with me so I didn't use this collar. So I listened to you.'"

Michelle went on to explain, "This dog had a reinforcement history with this collar and had a positive association with this collar. It only meant good things to him. What I learned was that the dog decides what is aversive and what is not. For this dog, the prong collar was not aversive, but everything else we tried to desensitize him to was. I told this story on a force-free trainer's column on Facebook and got kicked off the group. They just didn't understand that after three weeks I was forcing the dog to my prejudices about what the dog would see as using force and what was not. For me to be a force-free trainer I will not spend three weeks forcing the dog to fit into my mold of what I feel is aversive and what is not."

Do you have any employees or do you plan on having any?

"I have some apprentices and I have some interns. They are good, and when they finish they know that they can keep coming if they find the value in it."

Do you have any assistants, if so when were they added?

"If people have completed their apprentice or internship and I feel they are doing really well, I will let them become assistants."

How much help was your family in starting your business?

"I began using these other people seven years ago. But in the very beginning of the business I used my husband. The fact that my husband came to every class, and learned from me, helped convince me I could do that with other people. Well, he actually wasn't my husband at the time, he was my boyfriend."

What kind of family support did you have?

"Ironically, me and my future boyfriend had a couple of years where we were apart, but his mother actually came to several classes." As far as Michelle's immediate family? "I didn't have any financial support. I lived with my mom and my family gave me a lot of moral support."

How did you go about choosing your name?

"It was a process of experimenting and brainstorming with a lot of names. I ran ideas by my other dog friends. When I came up with Refined Canine, it just seemed right because we are refining dogs."

What kind of marketing do you do, or what did you feel your most successful marketing efforts were?

"When I first started, I got together a database of all the vet hospitals, then made a press kit to send. With the really local ones, I went in and introduced myself. I like to have some kind of written material beside my business cards. That way people have something they can use so maybe they will put that on their refrigerator. I have also offered free training for the vet staff. The vet staff can do one session for free or do one private lesson for free.

I find the front office people and vet staff are the ones who will or won't recommend you. That is where you want to build your relationship. I also offer free workshops for any vet who wants me to offer information on a topic their clients are really struggling with. I do this without charging for my time. I also put posters up in local community boards. I did try yellow pages and newspaper ads, but didn't have a good return for investment. Also ads in the church bulletin."

Do you sell dog equipment?

"I sold dog equipment from the beginning. Initially it wasn't much. I'd have leashes and collars on hand because a lot of people would come into class with a collar that was inappropriate, or too big or small for their dog. Or they'd have a retractable leash. When I crossed over to positive training, sometimes it was hard for people to find some of the equipment I recommended, so I'd have it there to sell."

What kind of facility do you have? Is this your final facility or a stepping stone?

Currently she has several facility options for training. "One is a community center where I do independent contracting for another dog trainer. I also do consultations in people's homes, and have a class outdoors that meets in different locations. This class meets in different places every week and is for people who have already gone through basic classes. Dogs can practice their skills in the real world so they will meet in places such as parks, the beach, and shopping centers. Dogs can walk by crowds of people, do polite greetings, and more."

Ultimately, the facility she'd like to have is one that has her own space. "I'd like to have a place where I can have a retail area, a quiet area for behavior consultations, a nice large indoor area for classes, and an outdoor play area for graduates."

Gail Fisher, Owner of All Dogs Gym

Do you do your own bookkeeping? Have you always done the bookkeeping this way? What fueled your decisions?

"Currently I don't do my own bookkeeping, but it was not always that way. When I began as a sole proprietor, I did do my own bookkeeping. Once my business grew, I quickly took on a good accountant and then moved on to hiring a bookkeeper. My advice to someone wanting to start her own business is to consider something that came as a gift to me from my sister-in-law who also owned a small business, a dance studio. We'd talk about our businesses and found they had a lot of parallels. As a gift, my sister-in-law gave me two hours with a business coach she was working with. In terms of learning to be a business person, this was the best gift any one could have given me. In our first session, the coach said to me, 'You know how to train dogs. My job is to teach you how to be a business person.' For the next eight years, I continued with monthly and sometimes even weekly phone meetings with him."

Is your business where you expected it?

"Oh no. As I said, my journey had a lot of serendipity. The location I leased for five years had just over 11,000 square feet. I thought it was perfect. All I had to do was put down dog mats. The first day in that building when I turned off the lights to close for the day, I thought I'd died and gone to heaven. This is exactly where I wanted to be and if I thought about my five-year plan, this was my fifteen-year plan. Then, three years later, I had outgrown it. Now my building is 25,000 square feet. So no, this is not what I ever expected."

How many years have you been in the dog training business?

"Over forty."

What are your future plans?

"To keep on keeping on. I want to keep learning, growing, and sharing my knowledge. The day I stop learning and growing I hope is my last day on earth."

When you began your business (or at any time), did you do a business plan? If not why?

"I did my first business plan when I wanted my own facility. At that time my office was at my home and my husband would come home and find me in tears with crumpled-up papers all around me because I couldn't figure out how I was going to instantly increase my classes from teaching eleven classes a week to twenty-five, because that was what I needed to pay the lease on the building. I did a business plan when I built my current building. I was looking for financing, and I needed a business plan for investors and the bank."

What were the biggest surprises with starting your business?

"I can't think of any surprises, since I really didn't have any expectations. I just knew I wanted to train dogs, so I set about learning how to do it, and continuing to learn and grow. Looking back on it from the vantage point of forty years' experience, I was truly blessed with some of the most wonderful teachers and mentors I met along the way who encouraged and guided my journey."

What were the biggest challenges with starting your business?

"The biggest challenge for me, as I think it is for anyone starting out as a dog trainer today, is gaining the experience necessary to be a true professional, and then working hard to develop a good reputation that encourages the paying customers—dog owners—that you're worth hiring. And in the meantime, finding a way to pay the bills. I think this is true of any entrepreneurial endeavor. Entrepreneurs are faced with challenges. Finding ways to overcome these challenges, whatever they may be, comes with the territory. My advice to someone starting out is to be realistic and honest with yourself. If you don't have the temperament and desire to take risks and work hard at your own business (not everyone does—and that's OK!), consider working for someone else who is willing to take the risks and take on the challenges."

Are you a sole proprietorship, LLC, partnership, or corporation? Has this status changed over the course of your business?

"I started as a sole proprietor and then moved to corporation. I never did an LLC. Years ago that option didn't exist."

Were there any unique customers or category of customer's issues you'd like to share an experience about?

"I try not to categorize our students and clients. I think it's critically important not to make assumptions and prejudge people. One of the most profound people lessons I had was from an old New Hampshire farmer that came to my classes with his Siberian Husky. During the first class session, for some reason, he hit his dog. The instructor, in a very quiet voice told him, 'Don't hit your dog. We don't allow hitting.' He completed that class (didn't walk out) but he called me the next day to complain, and said he wasn't coming back. The man explained that he had had dogs all his life. He said his dad had dogs on their farm, and they had wonderful relationships with them. He said, 'This is how I thought you trained a dog. I didn't know there was any other way.' He was almost in tears, and it was obvious he truly loved his dog. He simply didn't know there was any other way to train. So even with people we may tend to prejudge, it's important to keep in mind that they came to us to learn how to train their dogs and we need to find a way to help them do so."

Do you have any employees or do you plan on having any?

Since Gail already made it clear she has a very large facility with a lot of employees, her question was revamped a little and she was asked about when she took on assistants.

"I always like to have an assistant even if I only have three or four dogs in a class. When I am teaching a class and one of the dogs has an accident, I want an assistant to clean it up. I don't want the owner to have to clean it up, because the owner is already embarrassed. And if the owner is focused on cleaning the floor, then they can't be listening to what I am teaching. Between that and their embarrassment, that student isn't learning. It's also very helpful to have an extra set of eyes. From a business perspective, since being an assistant is one of the most important steps to becoming a trainer, this is how most of our trainers started out with us."

How much help was your family in starting your business?

"My first husband worked at his own job while I worked in the kennel and grew the dog business. His income was crucial to our support as I was getting started in my career. My current husband is totally supportive of my ventures, and is often helpful as a sounding board, or talking me down off the ceiling when things aren't going well."

How did you go about choosing your name?

"The name I started with was Canine Behavior Services. When I leased my first building, it had been a Gold's Gym prior to my renting it. My husband came up with the name All Dogs Gym—and I loved it from the very first time he said it."

What kind of marketing do you do, or what did you feel your most successful marketing efforts were?

"My newspaper column has been by far the most successful marketing tool for my business. I started out writing in the local free paper. Absolutely without question that is the thing that got my name known."

Do you sell dog equipment?

"When I purchased the boarding kennel, I sold dog food. I don't do that anymore for a variety of reasons. When I began my training classes, I priced my classes to include the collar and leashes I wanted students to use. If it broke they could buy a new one. At All Dogs Gym we have the space to do more retail. I don't necessarily recommend it for a new business since the overhead can be huge to have any range of inventory. For sole proprietor, you may want to keep it small like collars, leashes, and treats rather than carrying a wide range of items."

What kind of facility do you have? Is this your final facility or a stepping stone?

"Our 25,000-square-foot facility includes a 12,000-square-foot training arena, a three-room grooming salon suite, a doggy daycare caring for seventy-plus dogs a day, a seventy-five-run kennel, plus a professional career academy to learn dog training or dog grooming." As her history indicates she worked up into this facility over her forty-plus year career.

Sue Brown, Owner of Love My Dog Training and Light of Dog

Do you do your own bookkeeping? Have you always done the bookkeeping this way? What fueled your decisions?

"I do my own bookkeeping and always have. I have a background in accounting."

Is your business where you expected it?

"Yes."

How many years have you been in the dog training business?
"About sixteen."

Did you get to where you are now as quickly as you expected?
"I would have liked to have it happen sooner. But while working at the other job, I wanted to grow the business to a certain point before leaving the other career. The catch-22 is that you only have enough time to grow it to a certain point before you need to take that leap. I know I could have grown it faster if I'd have quit my other job sooner, but I still feel I grew it within the time I wanted to."

Is there a safety factor you were looking at?
"Part of my concern with quitting the other job was with health insurance. My husband had just gotten a job that had benefits, so this helped me be able to quit my job."

What are your future plans?
"Our new business we just started is called the Light of Dog. I have a new book (*Juvenile Delinquent Dogs*). I plan on keeping my dog business going while expanding my publications and online products."

When you began your business (or at any time), did you do a business plan? If not why?
"Yes."

What were the biggest surprises with starting your business?
"I don't know that there were any major surprises. I kind of knew what I was getting into. Between me working in the dog business previously, my business experience, and my husband's experience (he's worked with start-up businesses before) we pretty well knew what we were getting into."

Are you a sole proprietorship, LLC, partnership, or corporation? Has this status changed over the course of your business?
"Love My Dog Training is a sole proprietorship. Light of Dog is an LLC."

Were there any unique customers or category of customer's issues you'd like to share an experience about?
"I think as you get more practice with this business, you get a feel for who is going to

follow through on your training. When you first get started, sometimes you feel like you have to take on any customer you can get. But at some point, you discover that some customers can discourage you. If you are putting in your effort and they are not, they are not going to get any results. You have to be careful because you appear as if you are not successful when it is the customer who is not willing to do the work to get the results. So now, I try and communicate that they need some commitment and need to do work or they won't get anything out of this. Some people watch television shows and get the idea that they can solve a complex situation in thirty minutes. They just don't realize what goes on behind the scenes. So I try and help them to have realistic expectations and encourage them to be honest with themselves as to whether they are willing to put in the work."

Do you have any employees or do you plan on having any?
"No. In my accounting job I was a supervisor. I didn't want that with this job. Nor do I want to grow to the point that I'm so busy managing the business that I don't have time to do what I love to do.

Do you have any assistants, if so when were they added?
"I have none."

How much help was your family in starting your business?
"My husband has really helped in the business. He set up my website and helped with my business plan. He isn't a trainer, but he does help on the business side and the marketing. Without him, I'd had to have hired people to do those things and it would have cost a lot more."

What kind of family support did you have?
"My husband was very supportive about me leaving my other career to do this one."

How did you go about choosing your name?
"I spent a lot of time on that. I did find it fun playing around with a lot of different names. A lot of them got eliminated because someone else had the name or it was too similar to another name. I wanted something that was different than anything else."

What kind of marketing do you do, or what did you feel your most successful marketing efforts were?

"The majority of my clients come from vet referrals and client referrals. I do get some from Internet searches and referrals from retailers. To me, this business is best done through referrals. If you are going to be helping people with their dog, they will want to know you are worth working with. People who have a strong recommendation come to me already sold."

How do you network with those pet suppliers?

"I stop in and visit with them about once a month. I bring business cards and flyers. I also refer people to these suppliers when they have a new toy or equipment or better treats if a dog just isn't interested in the treats their owners are using. We help each other in our business. I generally don't send my clients to big-box stores. I send them to the independent retailers who really know about their products."

Do you sell dog equipment?

"No."

What kind of facility do you have?

"Most of my classes are at pet hospitals. With private consultations, I go to people's homes, or have a place at my home to work with dogs."

Is this your final facility or a stepping stone?

"I go back and forth about having my own space. Although there is some appeal, there is a lot to having your own facility. You have upkeep and more expenses. I'd rather keep things simple so I can better focus on my business."

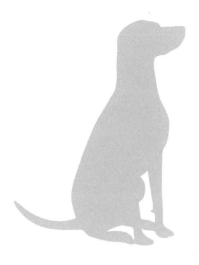

Agility Organizations

AKC (American Kennel Club)

akc.org

Has information on dog breeds, competition events, club search for training and services

NADAC (North American Dog Agility Council)

nadac.com

UKC (United Kennel Club)

ukcdogs.com

USDAA (United States Dog Agility Association)

usdaa.com

Behavioral Organizations

IAABC (International Association of Animal Behavior Consultants)

iaabc.org

Animal Behavior Society

animalbehaviorsociety.org

American College of Veterinary Behaviorists

dacvb.org

Certifications

American College of Veterinary Behaviorists:
DACVB—Diplomate of the American College of Veterinary Behaviorists

Animal Behavior Society:
ACAAB—Associate Certified Applied Animal Behaviorists
CAAB—Certified Applied Animal Behaviorist

Certification Council for Professional Dog Trainers:
CPDT-KA—Certified Professional Dog Trainer–Knowledge Assessed

International Association of Animal Behavior Consultants:
CABC—Certified Animal Behavior Consultant
CDBC—Certified Dog Behavior Consultant

International Association for the Study of Animal Behavior:
CCAB—Certified Clinical Behavior Consultant

Training Organizations

APDT (Association of Pet Dog Trainers)
apdt.com

NADOI (National Association of Dog Obedience Instructors)
nadoi.org
Certification for tracking, agility, and obedience. At this time Rally is not offered.

Appendix C: Resources

American Dog Owners Association: The ADOA is the nation's oldest and largest member-based organization representing dog owners for responsible dog ownership, adoa.org.

American Humane Association: This nonprofit membership organization was founded in 1877 and is dedicated to protecting children and animals, www.americanhumane.org.

Books and videos by Dr. Ian Dunbar as well as other noted publications.

Canine Performance Events: Sports help keep dogs active, www.k9cpe.com.

Certification Council for Professional Dog Trainers, www.ccpdt.org

Clicker Training: Check out Karen Pryor, www.clickertraining.com, and Gary Wilkes, www.clickandtreat.com.

Delta Society: This organization offers animal assistance to people in need, www.deltasociety.org.

E-trainingfordogs.com: Online dog training educational site offering a wide selection of webinars for the dog owner, dog trainer, breeder, and canine enthusiast, e-trainingfordogs.com.

International Association of Animal Behavior Consultants, www.iaabc.org

James and Kenneth Publications, www.jamesandkenneth.com.

Peggyswager.com: My website has discussions on several common dog behavior issues as well as several of my published articles.

Sirius Dog Training: Good information on basic dog training and dog training problems, www.siriuspup.com.

Tellington TTouch: A good sight to check out to find out more about this way of calming animals, www.ttouch.com.

Therapy Dog International, www.tdi-dog.org

What can we do for you?

Pet Dog Training - All Levels
Real Life Training Solutions
Group Classes
Private In-Home Lessons
Behavior Consultations
Specialty Training
Puppy Socialization
Behavior Assessments
Dogs & Storks™ Workshops
Dogs & Baby Connection™
AKC Canine Good Citizen® Evaluations
Pre-Adoption Consultations
Educational Events

Contact us today!

Never too soon...
Never too late...

Puppies are learning from the moment you bring them home and can begin coming to class as early as eight weeks old. Early training and socialization builds a strong foundation and is crucial in preventing behavior problems. The Refined Canine, LLC offers the area's ONLY off-leash puppy classes in the style of Dr. Ian Dunbar's Sirius® Puppy Training. Off-leash puppy classes teach puppies bite inhibition, impulse control, and good manners in a distracting environment. We teach puppies that good behavior works out better for them. This sets them up for good behavior on VOICE CONTROL!! Special collars or devices are not needed if you get into puppy classes early.

DO NOT WASTE PUPPYHOOD. The first 12 weeks can create a bomb-proof dog, or a time bomb. Puppies should've met 100 people in the first 8 weeks (most only meet 2-10), and ANOTHER 100 people before they're 12-weeks old! At 12 weeks old, the socialization window closes and each week it becomes exponentially more difficult to integrate your puppy into everyday life with humans!

AKC STAR PUPPY APPROVED CLASSES

You CAN teach an old dog new tricks! Older dogs excel in training; they want to learn and they are great learners! If you think your senior dog is too old to train, you're not giving your old friend enough credit.

**Family Focused Dog Training
& Behavior Consulting since 1997**

About us

Founded in 1997, The Refined Canine, LLC follows the philosophy of The LIMA Principle, which means we employ the Least Intrusive, Minimally Aversive methods needed to address training challenges based on each individual dog and his relationship with his people.

We offer a unique, family-focused approach to training and encourage all family members to participate, including children.

Michelle Douglas is a Certified Professional Dog Trainer (CPDT-KA) and Certified Dog Behavior Consultant (CDBC). Michelle is a past president of the Association of Pet Dog Trainers (APDT), the largest professional organization for pet dog trainers worldwide. She is a certified member of the International Association of Animal Behavior Consultants, an licensed educator for the Dogs & Storks™ and the Dog And Baby Connection™ programs, an AKC STAR PUPPY & Canine Good Citizen (CGC) Evaluator, and a Mentor Trainer for Animal Behavior College. Michelle has published several articles on various aspects of owning and training dogs, and is featured in the books Top Tips from Top Trainers (©2010 TFH Publications) and The Dog Trainer's Resource, The APDT Chronicle of the Dog Collection (©2006 Dogwise). Michelle is also a regular blogger on DogStarDaily.com, the website of Ian and Kelly Dunbar, and on several patch.com sites in southern New Haven County (Orange, Milford, Stratford).

The Refined Canine, LLC has been featured in the New Haven Register & Connecticut Post newspapers, on WFSB Channel 3 Eyewitness News & Cable Channel 12 Pet Talk, and Michelle is a regular guest on the Chaz & AJ morning show on 99.1 FM, WPLR, as well as the My Doggie Says radio program on KFNX 1100 out of Phoenix AZ.

Family Dog Training

Our group classes are designed to teach real life skills for pet dogs. We focus on building a strong relationship between the dog and his family, and creating a confident, well-mannered pet dog.

Classes offered include:
~Puppy Social Skills
~Basic Canine Life Skills
~Intermediate Life Skills
~Practicing in the REAL WORLD

Specialty & Advanced Classes:
~Snarky Dog
~Recall Refresher
~Common Problems
~CGC Preparatory Course
~Tricks for Treats
~Fun, Games & K9 Sports

Traveling Trainer - If you have a group of three or more dogs, and the space, I will come to you for a semi-private session at a reduced rate.

Dogs & Storks™ and Dog & Baby Connection™ workshops for preparation and successful parenting for dogs who live with kids!

Behavior Solutions
Educational Resources

Private Training
~In-home
~Tailored to your needs & schedule

Behavior Problem Consulting
~Personalized Written Plans
~Aggression
~Fear & Anxiety
~Destructive Behaviors
~Multi-Dog Solutions
~Multi-Species Solutions

Educational Workshops
~Schools & Libraries
~Bite Prevention
~Dog-related Events
~Simple techniques for Pet Professionals
~Life with Dogs for pet owners

Training the Trainer
~Apprentice & Mentoring Programs
~Lecturer / Speaker
~Trainer Roundtable Moderator

Index

A

ABS (Animal Behavior Society), 149
accounting. *See* bookkeeping and accounting; finances
accrual accounting, 54–55
advertising
    Google AdWords, 133
    mailing, 136–37
    via print, 135–36
    via veterinarians, groomers, doggy day care centers, 134–35
    word-of-mouth, 125–26
    See also marketing and public relations; websites
agility classes, 144–46
agility equipment, selling, 159–60
agility organizations, 151, 183
Aguiar, Dr. Cheryl Asmus, 153–54
All Dogs Gym, 9
American Express cards, 83
animal sensitivity, 2–3
answering machine, 28–29
APDT (Association of Pet Dog Trainers), 8, 20, 149
assets, balance sheet and, 60–61, 62
assistants
    friends as, 17–18
    qualifications for, 162–63
attire, dressing the part, 121–22
attorney, need for, 47–48. *See also* legal considerations
audience, knowing, 139
author, story of, 9–11
automobile
    insurance, 75
    mileage records/deductions, 57–58

B

balance sheet, 60–61, 62
banking
    checking/savings accounts, 80–81
    loan options, 89–91
behavioral organizations, 183
behaviorists, 148–49

bidding work out, 87–88
boarding dogs, 79
body language, canine, 15
bookkeeping and accounting
    big vs. small accounting firms, 53–54
    cash flow (cash) vs. accrual basis, 54–55
    choosing accountant, 51–54
    deducting business expenses, 59
    difference between, 49
    DIY or hiring out bookkeeping, 49–51
    expense analysis, 69–70, 71
    mileage deductions, 57–58
    paying employees, 164–65
    personal vs. business expenses, 59
    See also finances; financial statements; record keeping; taxes
booths, at shows/events, 136
breed education, 13–14
brochures, 133–34, 187
Brooks, Steve, 6–7
Brown, Sue, 6, 20–21, 179–82
business
    advantage of starting small, 159
    avoiding negative dog politics, 22
    building name in dog community, 21–22
    education, 72
    family, friends and, 16–18
    growing. *See* growing business
    home office considerations. *See* home office
    naming, 39–40
    neighbors and, 31–32
    networking in dog community, 18–21
    skill/knowledge requirements, 12–16. *See also* teaching
    structure options, 44–47
    support system, 16–17
business cards, 132–33

business interruption insurance, 77–78
business plan
    boarding dogs and, 79
    description of business, 34
    financial plan, 37–38. *See also* finances; financial statements
    marketing plan, 36–37, 139
    mission statement, 34–35
    organizational/management plans, 37
    overview and purpose, 33
    short- and long-term goals, 35–36

C

Calming Signals (Rugaas), 119
canine good citizen classes, 146
canine signals, 119
cash flow (cash) accounting, 54–55
cash flow projections, 66–68
cash flow reports, 61–64, 65
CCPDT (Certification Council for Professional Dog Trainers), 149
certificates of completion, 103, 104
certifications, for dog trainers, 149, 184
charge cards and credit cards
    accepting for payments, 83–85
    credit card financing, 92
    for expenses, 56, 82–83
checking account, 80–81
classes, teaching. *See* teaching
Clean Run Magazine, 121
clicker training, 118–19
client records
    future clients, 106
    keeping track of, 104–5, 106
    notes from private consultations, 96–99
    tracking paperwork, 96
clothing, appropriate, 121–22
Colorado Dog Trainer's Network, 20–21
communication
    canine body language and, 15
    fielding potential client questions, 106–8
    first impressions, 106–7

in-person tips, 108–9
keeping in touch, 105–6
keeping on track, 108
marketing and, tips, 140–41
phone use tips, 106–8
professional, cordial, 107–8, 109
talking with clients, 106–9
teaching, counseling, people skills
    and, 15–16
training tip, 109
competition, 140
completion, certificates of, 103, 104
computer
    accounting software, 58–59
    hardware requirements, 25–26
    keeping in touch via, 105–6
    tracking client/contact
        information, 104–5, 106
    using, 103–5
consultations. *See* dog consultations
contacts, tracking, 104–5, 106
contractors, hiring, 166–67
contracts, 100–103, 123–24
convenances, home office and, 30
corporations, 47
counseling skills, 15–16
crate training, 15
credit cards. *See* charge cards and
    credit cards

D
Dearth, Janice, 5–6, 19, 121, 150
description of business, 34
development stages of dogs, 14
dog community
    avoiding negative dog politics, 22
    building name in, 21–22
    mining future business, 23
    networking within, 18–21
dog consultations, 96–99, 122–23,
    146–47
dog training
    animal sensitivity and, 2–3
    assessing fit for you, 2–3
    behaviorists and, 148–49
    being successful at, 3
    book perspective, 1
    business of. *See* bookkeeping and
        accounting; business plan;
        finances; financial statements;
        record keeping; taxes
    certificates of completion, 103, 104
    certifications, 149, 184
    class syllabus and contract,
        100–103

consultations and, 96–99, 122–23,
    146–47
contract, 123–24
difference between professional
    trainer and want-to-be, 150
finding niche in, 4–5
need for, 3–4
reasons for pursuing, 1–2
reference library, 116–21
schools, 151–52. *See also* education
skills and training for. *See*
    education; skill/knowledge
    requirements; teaching
success stories, 5–11
doggy day care, advertising via, 134
The Dog's Mind (Fogle and Wilson),
    117, 118
domain names, 43
Don't Shoot the Dog (Pryor), 118–19
doo-doo, dealing with, 116
Douglas, Michelle, 7–8, 171–76
dressing the part, 121–22
drop-in classes, 145

E
education
    business-related, 72
    certifications, 149, 184
    dog training schools, 151–52
    e-training, 153–57
    PetSmart or Petco, 152–53
    Rally and Agility organizations, 151
    See also skill/knowledge
        requirements; teaching
employees
    adding, 160–64
    avoiding payroll, 165
    correcting problems with, 169
    dog assistant qualifications, 162–63
    family factor, 167–68
    forms/paperwork for, 164
    hiring contractors instead of,
        166–67
    hiring through temporary agency,
        165
    hourly, 164–65
    interviewing, 161–62
    motivating to do their best,
        168–70
    non-competitive clauses, 163–64
    paying, 164–65
    relationships with, 167–68
    staff meetings for, 169–70
    training/acquiring another
        trainer, 163

Employer Identification Number (EIN),
    70
equipment, for home office, 25–29,
    93–94
equipment, for training area, 115–16
equipment, selling, 159–60
e-training, 153–57
events, booths at, 136
expenses. *See* bookkeeping and
    accounting; finances; record
    keeping; taxes

F
Facebook, 126–30
family and friends
    explaining responsibilities to,
        110
    office hours and, 109–10
    relationships, business and, 17
    support and involvement, 16–18
fax machine, 26
filing cabinets, 27
finances
    assessing regularly, 69
    bidding work out, 87–88
    borrowing money. *See* loans
    business structure options and,
        44–47
    checking/savings accounts, 80–81
    checks as receipts, 81
    cost of doing business, 86–89
    expense analysis, 69–70, 71
    investor money and, 92–93
    perspective on, 69
    plan for, 37–38
    working with accountant, 69
    See also bookkeeping and
        accounting; charge cards and
        credit cards; record keeping;
        taxes
financial statements, 60–68
    about: overview of, 60
    assets, liabilities and, 60–61
    balance sheet, 60–61, 62
    cash flow projections, 66–68
    cash flow reports, 61–64, 65
    income statement, 61
    inventory and, 65
    when to generate, 64
    See also bookkeeping and
        accounting; record keeping;
        taxes
first impressions, 106–7
Fisher, Gail, 8–9, 151–52, 176–79
friends. *See* family and friends

G
gift certificates, 138
goals, short- and long-term, 35–36
good citizen classes, 146
Google AdWords, 133
groomers, advertising via, 134
growing business, 158–70
    advantage of starting small, 158
    health insurance, benefits and, 167
    hiring subcontractors/independent
        contractors, 166–67
    offering other dog services, 160
    selling equipment, 159–60
    See also employees

H
health, canine, 15
health insurance, 167
home office
    about: overview of, 24
    deduction for, 59–60
    dog area and, 29
    equipment, 25–29, 93–94
    functions and benefits, 25
    neighbors and, 31–32
    office hours, 109–10
    questions to answer about, 24–25
    setting up, 24–25
    See also legal considerations
hours, office, 109–10
housetraining, 14–15

I
IAABC (International Association of
    Animal Behavior), 149
image and logo, 40–41
income statement, 61
income taxes, 71–72
independent consulting, 122–23, 146–47
I-9 form, 164
insurance
    about: overview of, 73
    agent interview, 76–77
    automobile, 75
    business interruption, 77–78
    health, 167
    homeowner extensions or
        independent policies, 73–74
    independent agent for, 79
    liability, 75–77
    workman's compensation, 78,
        165, 167
Internet presence
    blogging, 132

Google AdWords, 133
    online forums, 19–20
    social media, 126–32
    See also websites
interviewing prospective employees,
    161–62
inventory
    accounting considerations, 65
    selling merchandise, 94
investor money, 92–93
IP addresses, 43

K
K9U, 6–7

L
legal considerations
    business structure options, 44–47
    convenances and zoning, 30
    health department/state
        regulations, 31
    licensing and permits, 31
    non-competitive clauses, 163–64
    why you need attorney, 47–48
    See also insurance; taxes
liabilities, balance sheet and, 60–61, 62
liability insurance, 75–77
library, reference, 116–21
licensing and permits, 31
LLCs, 46
loans
    bank, 89–91
    considerations for taking, 89
    from government, 91
    secured, 90
    unsecured, 90–91
logo and image, 40–41
Love My Dog Training, 6

M
magazines, 121, 135
mailings, 136–37
management plan, 37
marketing and public relations, 125–41
    about: overview/summary of, 125, 141
    art of a sale, 140
    basis of, 139–40
    blogging, 132
    booths at shows/events, 136
    building name in dog community,
        21–22
    building word of mouth, 125–26
    business cards and brochures,
        132–34, 187
    communication tips, 140–41

    distinction from competition, 140
    dressing the part, 121–22
    executing in stages, 139
    gift certificates, 138
    knowing your audience, 139
    logo, image and, 40–41
    mining future business, 23, 137–38
    naming business, 39–40
    plan, 36–37, 139
    See also advertising; Internet
        presence; networking; websites
Medicare tax, 72
medicine, canine, 15
merchandise
    guidelines for selling, 94
    inventory accounting
        considerations, 65
    pricing services and, 94–95
mileage, tracking, 57–58
mission statement, 34–35
motivating employees, 168–70

N
name, building, 21–22
naming business, 39–40
need, for dog training, 3–4
neighbors, consideration for, 31–32
networking
    creating network, 20–21
    importance of, 18–19
    online forums for, 19–20
    in person, 20
niche, finding, 4–5
non-competitive clauses, 163–64
notes, from private consultations, 96–99
nutrition, canine, 15

O
obedience classes, 143–44
office. *See* home office
online forums. *See* Internet presence
online training, 153–57
organizational/management plans, 37
organizations
    agility, 151, 183
    associations, 183, 184
    behavioral, 183
    certifications by, 149, 184
    promoting specific disciplines, 150
    Rally, 151
    training, 184

P
pack behaviors, 14
partnerships, 44–46

paying employees, 164–65
people skills, 15–16
permits and licensing, 31
PetSmart and Petco education, 152–53
petty cash, 57
phone book advertising, 135–36
phones
    fielding potential client questions,
        106–8
    first impressions and, 106–7
    talking with clients, 106–8
    types and considerations, 27–29
    use/etiquette tips, 106–8
politics (negative), avoiding, 22
pricing, 94–95
print advertising, 135–36
printers, 26
private consultations. See dog
        consultations
puppy classes, 142–43

Q
questions and answers, 171–82

R
*The Rally Course Book: A Guide to AKC
        Rally Courses* (Dearth), 121
Rally organizations, 151
*Reaching the Dog's Mind, Clicker
        Training . . .* (Pryor), 119
receipts, tracking, 55–56, 81
record keeping, 55–60
    charge/credit cards for, 56, 82–85
    for client information. See client
        records
    home office deduction, 59–60
    keeping current, 54
    mileage, 57–58
    petty cash, 57
    receipts, 55–56, 81
    software/programs for, 58–59
    See also bookkeeping and
        accounting; finances; taxes
reference library, 116–21
Refined Canine, 8
resources, 185–86

S
sales
    art of, 140
    selling equipment, 159–60
    selling merchandise, 94
    See also advertising; Internet
        presence; marketing and public
        relations; networking; websites

sales tax, 70–71
savings account, 81
S-Corporations, 46–47
self-employment taxes, 72
services, other, 160
shows, booths at, 136
signals, canine, 119
skill/knowledge requirements, 12–16
    about: overview of, 12
    breed education, 13–14
    canine body language, 15
    canine health/nutrition/medicine,
        15
    counseling/interpersonal skills,
        15–16
    dog development stages, 14
    housetraining/crate training, 14–15
    pack behaviors, 14
    places to learn, 147–48
    running your business, 16
    See also education; teaching
small business loans. See loans
social media, 126–32
Social Security tax, 72
software, for record keeping, 58–59
sole proprietorships, 44
staff. See employees
staff meetings, 169–70
storage space, home office, 27, 29
storage unit conversion, 88–89
Stowers, Dennis, 76–77
subcontractors, hiring, 166–67
success
    requirements for, 3
    stories, of trainers, 5–11
supplies, buying, 93–94
support system, family/friends and,
        16–18. See also networking
syllabus and contract, 100–103

T
taxes, 70–72
    deducting business expenses, 59
    employee forms/paperwork (I-9,
        W-4), 164
    federal identification number
        (EIN), 70
    home office deduction, 59–60
    income, 71–72
    mileage deductions, 57–58
    personal vs. business expenses,
        59
    quarterly, paying, 72

sales, 70–71
self-employment (Social Security
        and Medicare), 72
withholding, 164–65
teaching
    agility classes, 144–46
    behaviorists and, 148–49
    canine good citizen classes, 146
    classes, qualifications for, 142–47
    drop-in classes, 145
    independent consulting and, 146–
        47. See also dog consultations
    obedience classes, 143–44
    offering other dog services, 160
    places to learn skills, 147–48
    puppy classes, 142–43
    skill/knowledge requirements, 16,
        143–44, 145–46, 147
Tellington TTouch, 119–21
temporary employees, 165
trainer, training/acquiring, 163
training. See dog training; teaching
training area
    brainstorming needs list, 111–13
    creating, 111–14
    dealing with doo-doo, 116
    equipment for, 115–16
    facility considerations, 115
    intermediate classroom, 114
    renting facilities, 114–15
    size requirements, 113–14
Twitter, 131–32

W
websites
    addresses (URLs), obtaining, 41–43
    designing, insider's perspective,
        127–29
    domain names, 43
    hosts, 43
    importance of, 126
    IP addresses, 43
    keeping current, 126
    online forums and, 19–20
W-4 form, 164
word-of-mouth advertising, 125–26
workman's compensation insurance,
        78, 165, 167

Y
YouTube, 130–31

Z
zoning issues, 30

About the Author

Peggy Swager began her animal training adventures in the 1970s as she graduated with a BS in biology and worked for several years with animals to gain the credentials to call herself a behaviorist. In the 1990s Peggy intensified her studies for working with dogs. Over the years, she has trained, shown (obedience, go-to-ground, conformation, agility), taught dog classes (puppy classes, obedience, agility), and consulted on problem dog behaviors. She currently has a dog consultation business where she helps dog owners resolve unwanted and difficult behaviors. She also is working with some of the more problematic dogs from National Mill Dog Rescue. Peggy has written about some of her dog training experiences for *Dog World, AKC Gazette, OffLead Magazine,* and many other magazines. She has had several articles nominated for awards, two of which won in the DWAA (Dog Writer's Association of America) contest. She is the author of two breed books on Jack Russell/Parson Russell Terriers and a breed book on Boston Terriers. Her dog training book, *Training the Hard to Train Dog,* has received strong reviews. She brings her vast years of experience to this book to help people learn where to begin, how to hone their skills, and grow their business.